A Commentary on the United Nations Convention
on the Rights of the Child

Editors

André Alen, Johan Vande Lanotte, Eugeen Verhellen,
Fiona Ang, Eva Berghmans and Mieke Verheyde

Articles 43-45

The UN Committee on the Rights of the Child

By

Mieke Verheyde

Researcher at the Human Rights Centre, Ghent University, Belgium

and

Geert Goedertier

Legal secretary at the Belgian Constitutional Court
Researcher at the Human Rights Centre, Ghent University, Belgium

MARTINUS NIJHOFF PUBLISHERS
LEIDEN • BOSTON
2006

This book is printed on acid-free paper.

A Cataloging-in-Publication record for this book is available from the Library of Congress.

Cite as: M. Verheyde and G. Goedertier, "Articles 43–45: The UN Committee on the Rights of the Child", in: A. Alen, J. Vande Lanotte, E. Verhellen, F. Ang, E. Berghmans and M. Verheyde (Eds.) *A Commentary on the United Nations Convention on the Rights of the Child* (Martinus Nijhoff Publishers, Leiden 2006).

ISSN 1574-8626
ISBN 90-04-14731-4

CONTENTS

LIST OF ABBREVIATIONS

CAT	International Convention against Torture
CAT Committee	UN Committee against Torture
CCPR	International Covenant on Civil and Political Rights
CEDAW	International Convention on the Elimination of All Forms of Discrimination against Women
CEDAW Committee	UN Committee on the Elimination of All Forms of Discrimination against Women
CERD	International Convention on the Elimination of All Forms of Racial Discrimination
CERD Committee	UN Committee on the Elimination of All Forms of Racial Discrimination
CESCR	International Covenant on Economic, Social and Cultural Rights
CESCR Committee	UN Committee on Economic, Social and Cultural Rights
CMW	International Convention on the Protection of the Rights of All Migrant Workers and Members of their Families
CMW Committee	UN Committee on the Protection of the Rights of All Migrant Workers and Members of their Families
CRC	International Convention on the Rights of the Child
CRC Committee	UN Committee on the Rights of the Child
ILO	International Labour Organization
NGO	Non-governmental organisation
UN	United Nations
UNESCO	United Nations Educational, Scientific and Cultural Organisation
UNHCR	United Nations High Commissioner for Refugees
UNICEF	United Nations Children's Fund
WHO	World Health Organization

AUTHOR BIOGRAPHY

Mieke Verheyde is a Belgian researcher at the Human Rights Centre of Ghent University (Belgium). She is involved in an interdisciplinary inter-university research project on the UN Convention on the Rights of the Child and conducts comparative research on the protection of children's rights by the European Court of Human Rights and the US Supreme Court. Previously, she worked for two years as a researcher on women's rights issues in the Cabinet of the Belgian federal minister of employment and labour, and as a member of the Equal Opportunities Department of the Belgian federal ministry of employment and labour. She studied law at the University of Leuven (Belgium), obtained an LL.M. at the University of Stellenbosch (South Africa) and a European Master's Degree in Human Rights and Democratisation at the University of Padova (Italy).

Geert Goedertier is Belgian by nationality and studied law at Ghent University (Belgium). He is a legal secretary at the Belgian Constitutional Court and researcher at the Public Law Department/Human Rights Centre of Ghent University. His research covers most areas of human rights law and Belgian constitutional law. He is the author of numerous publications in this field.

TEXT OF ARTICLES 43, 44, AND 45

ARTICLE 43

1. For the purpose of examining the progress made by States Parties in achieving the realization of the obligations undertaken in the present Convention, there shall be established a Committee on the Rights of the Child, which shall carry out the functions hereinafter provided.

2. The Committee shall consist of ten experts of high moral standing and recognized competence in the field covered by this Convention. The members of the Committee shall be elected by States Parties from among their nationals and shall serve in their personal capacity, consideration being given to equitable geographical distribution, as well as to the principal legal systems. (amendement)

3. The members of the Committee shall be elected by secret ballot from a list of persons nominated by States Parties. Each State Party may nominate one person from among its own nationals.

4. The initial election to the Committee shall be held no later than six months after the date of the entry into force of the present Convention and thereafter every second year. At least four months before the date of

ARTICLE 43

1. Aux fins d'examiner les progrès accomplis par les Etats parties dans l'exécution des obligations contractées par eux en vertu de la présente Convention, il est institué un Comité des droits de l'enfant qui s'acquitte des fonctions définies ci-après.

2. Le Comité se compose de dix experts de haute moralité et possédant une compétence reconnue dans le domaine visé par la présente Convention. Ses membres sont élus par les Etats parties parmi leurs ressortissants et siègent à titre personnel, compte tenu de la nécessité d'assurer une répartition géographique équitable et eu égard aux principaux systèmes juridiques. (amendement)

3. Les membres du Comité sont élus au scrutin secret sur une liste de personnes désignées par les Etats parties. Chaque Etat partie peut désigner un candidat parmi ses ressortissants.

4. La première élection aura lieu dans les six mois suivant la date d'entrée en vigueur de la présente Convention. Les élections auront lieu ensuite tous les deux ans. Quatre mois au moins avant la date de chaque

each election, the Secretary-General of the United Nations shall address a letter to States Parties inviting them to submit their nominations within two months. The Secretary-General shall subsequently prepare a list in alphabetical order of all persons thus nominated, indicating States Parties which have nominated them, and shall submit it to the States Parties to the present Convention.

5. The elections shall be held at meetings of States Parties convened by the Secretary-General at United Nations Headquarters. At those meetings, for which two thirds of States Parties shall constitute a quorum, the persons elected to the Committee shall be those who obtain the largest number of votes and an absolute majority of the votes of the representatives of States Parties present and voting.

6. The members of the Committee shall be elected for a term of four years. They shall be eligible for re-election if renominated. The term of five of the members elected at the first election shall expire at the end of two years; immediately after the first election, the names of these five members shall be chosen by lot by the Chairman of the meeting.

7. If a member of the Committee dies or resigns or declares that for any other cause he or she can no longer perform the duties of the Committee, the State Party which nominated the member shall appoint

élection, le Secrétaire général de l'Organisation des Nations Unies invitera par écrit les Etats parties à proposer leurs candidats dans un délai de deux mois. Le Secrétaire général dressera ensuite la liste alphabétique des candidats ainsi désignés, en indiquant les Etats parties qui les ont désignés, et la communiquera aux Etats parties à la présente Convention.

5. Les élections ont lieu lors des réunions des Etats parties, convoquées par le Secrétaire général au Siège de l'Organisation des Nations Unies. A ces réunions, pour lesquelles le quorum est constitué par les deux tiers des Etats parties, les candidats élus au Comité sont ceux qui obtiennent le plus grand nombre de voix et la majorité absolue des voix des représentants des Etats parties présents et votants.

6. Les membres du Comité sont élus pour quatre ans. Ils sont rééligibles si leur candidature est présentée à nouveau. Le mandat de cinq des membres élus lors de la première élection prend fin au bout de deux ans. Les noms de ces cinq membres seront tirés au sort par le président de la réunion immédiatement après la première élection.

7. En cas de décès ou de démission d'un membre du Comité, ou si, pour toute autre raison, un membre déclare ne plus pouvoir exercer ses fonctions au sein du Comité, l'Etat partie qui avait présenté sa candidature nomme

another expert from among its nationals to serve for the remainder of the term, subject to the approval of the Committee.

8. The Committee shall establish its own rules of procedure.

9. The Committee shall elect its officers for a period of two years.

10. The meetings of the Committee shall normally be held at United Nations Headquarters or at any other convenient place as determined by the Committee. The Committee shall normally meet annually. The duration of the meetings of the Committee shall be determined, and reviewed, if necessary, by a meeting of the States Parties to the present Convention, subject to the approval of the General Assembly.

11. The Secretary-General of the United Nations shall provide the necessary staff and facilities for the effective performance of the functions of the Committee under the present Convention.

12. With the approval of the General Assembly, the members of the Committee established under the present Convention shall receive emoluments from United Nations resources on such terms and conditions as the Assembly may decide.

un autre expert parmi ses ressortissants pour pourvoir le poste ainsi vacant jusqu'à l'expiration du mandat correspondant, sous réserve de l'approbation du Comité.

8. Le Comité adopte son règlement intérieur.

9. Le Comité élit son bureau pour une période de deux ans.

10. Les réunions du Comité se tiennent normalement au Siège de l'Organisation des Nations Unies, ou en tout autre lieu approprié déterminé par le Comité. Le Comité se réunit normalement chaque année. La durée de ses sessions est déterminée et modifiée, si nécessaire, par une réunion des Etats parties à la présente Convention, sous réserve de l'approbation de l'Assemblée générale.

11. Le Secrétaire général de l'Organisation des Nations Unies met à la disposition du Comité le personnel et les installations qui lui sont nécessaires pour s'acquitter efficacement des fonctions qui lui sont confiées en vertu de la présente Convention.

12. Les membres du Comité institué en vertu de la présente Convention reçoivent, avec l'approbation de l'Assemblée générale, des émoluments prélevés sur les ressources de l'Organisation des Nations Unies dans les conditions et selon les modalités fixées par l'Assemblée générale.

ARTICLE 44

1. States Parties undertake to submit to the Committee, through the Secretary-General of the United Nations, reports on the measures they have adopted which give effect to the rights recognized herein and on the progress made on the enjoyment of those rights

(a) Within two years of the entry into force of the Convention for the State Party concerned;

(b) Thereafter every five years.

2. Reports made under the present article shall indicate factors and difficulties, if any, affecting the degree of fulfilment of the obligations under the present Convention. Reports shall also contain sufficient information to provide the Committee with a comprehensive understanding of the implementation of the Convention in the country concerned.

3. A State Party which has submitted a comprehensive initial report to the Committee need not, in its subsequent reports submitted in accordance with paragraph 1 (b) of the present article, repeat basic information previously provided.

4. The Committee may request from States Parties further information relevant to the implementation of the Convention.

ARTICLE 44

1. Les Etats parties s'engagent à soumettre au Comité, par l'entremise du Secrétaire général de l'Organisation des Nations Unies, des rapports sur les mesures qu'ils auront adoptées pour donner effet aux droits reconnus dans la présente Convention et sur les progrès réalisés dans la jouissance de ces droits :

(a) Dans les deux ans à compter de la date de l'entrée en vigueur de la présente Convention pour les Etats parties intéressés;

(b) Par la suite, tous les cinq ans.

2. Les rapports établis en application du présent article doivent, le cas échéant, indiquer les facteurs et les difficultés empêchant les Etats parties de s'acquitter pleinement des obligations prévues dans la présente Convention. Ils doivent également contenir des renseignements suffisants pour donner au Comité une idée précise de l'application de la Convention dans le pays considéré.

3. Les Etats parties ayant présenté au Comité un rapport initial complet n'ont pas, dans les rapports qu'ils lui présentent ensuite conformément à l'alinéa b du paragraphe 1 du présent article, à répéter les renseignements de base antérieurement communiqués.

4. Le Comité peut demander aux Etats parties tous renseignements complémentaires relatifs à l'application de la Convention.

5. The Committee shall submit to the General Assembly, through the Economic and Social Council, every two years, reports on its activities.

6. States Parties shall make their reports widely available to the public in their own countries.

ARTICLE 45

In order to foster the effective implementation of the Convention and to encourage international co-operation in the field covered by the Convention:

(a) The specialized agencies, the United Nations Children's Fund, and other United Nations organs shall be entitled to be represented at the consideration of the implementation of such provisions of the present Convention as fall within the scope of their mandate. The Committee may invite the specialized agencies, the United Nations Children's Fund and other competent bodies as it may consider appropriate to provide expert advice on the implementation of the Convention in areas falling within the scope of their respective mandates. The Committee may invite the specialized agencies, the United Nations Children's Fund, and other United Nations organs to submit reports on the implementation of the Convention in areas falling within the scope of their activities;

5. Le Comité soumet tous les deux ans à l'Assemblée générale, par l'entremise du Conseil économique et social, un rapport sur ses activités.

6. Les Etats parties assurent à leurs rapports une large diffusion dans leur propre pays.

ARTICLE 45

Pour promouvoir l'application effective de la Convention et encourager la coopération internationale dans le domaine visé par la Convention :

(a) Les institutions spécialisées, le Fonds des Nations Unies pour l'enfance et d'autres organes des Nations Unies ont le droit de se faire représenter lors de l'examen de l'application des dispositions de la présente Convention qui relèvent de leur mandat. Le Comité peut inviter les institutions spécialisées, le Fonds des Nations Unies pour l'enfance et tous autres organismes qu'il jugera appropriés à donner des avis spécialisés sur l'application de la Convention dans les domaines qui relèvent de leurs mandats respectifs. Il peut inviter les institutions spécialisées, le Fonds des Nations Unies pour l'enfance et d'autres organes des Nations Unies à lui présenter des rapports sur l'application de la Convention dans les secteurs qui relèvent de leur domaine d'activité;

(b) The Committee shall transmit, as it may consider appropriate, to the specialized agencies, the United Nations Children's Fund and other competent bodies, any reports from States Parties that contain a request, or indicate a need, for technical advice or assistance, along with the Committee's observations and suggestions, if any, on these requests or indications;

(c) The Committee may recommend to the General Assembly to request the Secretary-General to undertake on its behalf studies on specific issues relating to the rights of the child;

(d) The Committee may make suggestions and general recommendations based on information received pursuant to articles 44 and 45 of the present Convention. Such suggestions and general recommendations shall be transmitted to any State Party concerned and reported to the General Assembly, together with comments, if any, from States Parties.

(b) Le Comité transmet, s'il le juge nécessaire, aux institutions spécialisées, au Fonds des Nations Unies pour l'enfance et aux autres organismes compétents tout rapport des Etats parties contenant une demande ou indiquant un besoin de conseils ou d'assistance techniques, accompagné, le cas échéant, des observations et suggestions du Comité touchant ladite demande ou indication;

(c) Le Comité peut recommander à l'Assemblée générale de prier le Secrétaire général de procéder pour le Comité à des études sur des questions spécifiques touchant les droits de l'enfant;

(d) Le Comité peut faire des suggestions et des recommandations d'ordre général fondées sur les renseignements reçus en application des articles 44 et 45 de la présente Convention. Ces suggestions et recommandations d'ordre général sont transmises à tout Etat partie intéressé et portées à l'attention de l'Assemblée générale, accompagnées, le cas échéant, des observations des Etats parties.

CHAPTER ONE

INTRODUCTION*

1. The implementation of the rights enshrined in the UN Convention on the Rights of the Child[1] is primarily a matter of national legislation, policy and litigation.[2] By ratifying a legally binding instrument, the States Parties indeed have assumed the responsibility to give effect to the Convention's provisions. However, the text of the CRC reveals that the implementation of its standards should not be considered solely as a national concern. Articles 43 to 45 of the CRC provide for an implementation system on the international level

---

* By January 2005, with the exception of a more recent reference under footnote 32.
[1] Hereinafter referred to as 'the CRC' or 'the Convention'. The Convention was adopted on 20 November 1989 and entered into force on 2 September 1990. As of January 2005, the CRC has been signed and ratified by 192 States, which makes it almost universal (Somalia and the United States are the only States that signed the Convention without ratifying it). By General Assembly resolution A/RES54/263 of 25 May 2000 two optional protocols to the CRC were adopted: (1) Optional Protocol on the involvement of children in armed conflict, ratified by 86 countries (as of November 2004), entered into force on 12 February 2002; and (2) Optional Protocol on the sale of children, child prostitution and child pornography, ratified by 85 States (as of November 2004), entered into force on 18 January 2002.
[2] There exists a consensus that the implementation of international human rights should primarily be done through action at the national level. This means *in the first place* the inclusion of the international human rights provisions in the national legal order by adopting national legislation. This is essential in States belonging to the 'dualistic school', which proclaims that an obligation under international law has effect in the domestic legal system only after it has been transposed into national law. The effect and meaning of a treaty only derives from domestic legal provisions. Also in States belonging to the 'monistic school', implementation of international human rights standards sometimes requires action from the national legislator. Although this school sees the law as a whole and therefore considers international legal rules as part of that one legal system which applies to all legal subjects in that country, not all provisions of a treaty acquire a self – executing force. This implies that provisions without self – executing character should be translated into national provisions in order to be enforceable, *i.e.* so that they can be invoked in a domestic court. Furthermore, sometimes legislative reform is necessary in order to comply with the international treaty. *In the second place*, States must attune their national policy to the ratified provisions of a treaty. *In the third place*, the domestic courts can play a significant role in the implementation of international human rights law. See *inter alia* L.F. Zwaak, *International Human rights procedures – Petitioning the ECHR, CCPR and CERD* (Utrecht, Ars Aequi Libri, 1991), V and T. Opsahl, 'Instruments of Implementation of Human Rights', *Human Rights Law Journal* 10, No 1–2, 1989, p. 32: 'One should never forget that national implementation must be the alpha and omega'.

performed by the Committee on the Rights of the Child.[3] The latter's existence is in the first place based on the belief that absence of an international system of *control* would most probably lead to failure by the States Parties to fulfil their CRC obligations. In the second place, the CRC Committee was established to *assist* the governments, to strengthen the national mechanisms in the gradual process of realising the rights of the child.

2. The present text is a commentary on this international implementation system[4] and is part of the series 'A Commentary on the United Nations Convention on the Rights of the Child'. Contrary to the other volumes of this series, this volume does not deal with the substantive rights of the CRC but concerns its procedural provisions. We therefore chose to structure the text differently from the other volumes as we think it will serve the reader better. The text mainly provides an overview of the key activities of the CRC Committee. A special emphasis is put on the reporting procedure, which constitutes the Committee's basic supervisory tool. Throughout the paper and especially in the last chapter the effectiveness of the reporting procedure is touched upon.

---

[3] Hereafter referred to as 'the CRC Committee' or 'the Committee'.

[4] The terms 'implementation' and 'monitoring' in this paper are used in the way Parmentier defines them. In his view 'implementation' is broader than 'monitoring' and can be defined as 'the totality of actions undertaken to give effect to human rights standards, (a) at distinct levels of interaction, (b) by a number of different agents, (c) who can make use of different strategies'. The author considers 'monitoring' as 'only one type of human rights implementation, in which actions of certain agents are evaluated against the background of their human rights obligations'. This paper deals with an international monitoring mechanism where an international supervisory body, *i.e.* the committee, supervises the application of the CRC's provisions by the States Parties. (S. Parmentier, 'The Significance of Mechanisms to Monitor Human Rights at the International Level', in: E. Verhellen and A. Weyts (eds.), *Understanding Children's Rights-2003* (Ghent, Children's Rights Centre, Ghent University, 2004), p. 350.

CHAPTER TWO

THE CRC COMMITTEE SITUATED WITHIN THE UNITED NATIONS HUMAN RIGHTS' APPARATUS

3. Like most institutions dealing with human rights at the international level, the CRC Committee operates within the framework of the United Nations. The UN activities in the domain of human rights are carried out by a rather opaque ensemble of procedures and organs.[5]

4. In general, the UN organs are classified on the ground of their juridical basis: 'charter-based organs' on the one hand and 'treaty-based organs' on the other hand.[6] The first group entails the six principal organs,[7] the functional commissions of the Economic and Social Council[8] and the sub-commissions founded by these functional commissions.[9] Among those, the Commission on Human Rights is the central human rights body. The 'treaty-based organs'

---

[5] For an overview of the UN human rights regime: see M. Nowak, *Introduction to the International Human Rights Regime* (Leiden/Boston, Martinus Nijhoff Publishers, 2003), pp. 73–156. For an overview of the UN activities in the domain of children's rights: see G. Van Bueren, *The International Law on the Rights of the Child* (The Hague, Martinus Nijhoff Publishers, 1998), pp. 383–401.

[6] Ph. Alston, 'Appraising the United Nations Human Rights Regime', in: Ph. Alston (ed.), *The United Nations and Human Rights. A Critical Appraisal* (Oxford, Clarendon Press, 1992), pp. 4–5.

[7] The General Assembly, the Economic and Social Council, the Security Council, the International Court of Justice, the Trusteeship Council and the Secretariat (Secretary-General).

The 'High Commissioner for Human Rights' (a function created by the General Assembly in December 1993) carries out the *good offices* – function in the field of human rights on behalf of the Secretary-General. He or she is the UN official with principal responsibility for human rights activities and is responsible for promoting and protecting human rights all over the world (currently, Louise Arbour takes up the mandate of High Commissioner). The 'Office of the High Commissioner for Human Rights' (former Centre for Human Rights) implements the policies of the High Commissioner. On the functioning of this office and the role of the High Commissioner, see B.G. Ramcharan, *The United Nations High Commissioner for Human Rights, the Challenges of International Protection* (The Hague, Kluwer Law International, 2002), 250 p.

[8] There are nine functional commissions: Statistical Commission, Commission on Population and Development, Commission for Social Development, Commission on Human Rights, Commission on the Status of Women, Commission on Narcotic Drugs, Commission on Science and Technology for Development, Commission on Crime Prevention and Criminal Justice and Commission on Sustainable Development.

[9] The most important one is the Sub-Commission on Prevention of Discrimination and Protection of Minorities.

are the bodies that were established by specific treaties.[10] The CRC Committee is classified under this group. According to Alston, both types of organs mainly distinguish themselves from each other as far as their mandate and attitude with regard to the States are concerned.[11] The 'treaty-based organs' bear the responsibility for monitoring the implementation of the provisions of the treaties concerned. The 'charter-based organs' have a much broader mandate to promote awareness, to foster respect, and to respond to violations of human rights standards. Furthermore, the 'treaty-based organs' mainly take a non-conflicting stance vis-à-vis the States Parties, whereas the 'charter-based organs' take strongly conflicting stances whenever needed. Another distinction between both types of organs is that 'treaty-based organs' are expert bodies with members serving in their personal capacity whereas most of[12] the 'charter-based organs' are political institutions, consisting of government representatives, who act in accordance with their government's policies.

5. These bodies have a set of procedures at their disposal, such as State reporting procedures,[13] inter-state communications procedures,[14] individual communications procedures,[15] country procedures,[16] thematic

---

[10] The Committee on Elimination of Racial Discrimination, the Committee on Elimination of Discrimination against Women, the Human Rights Committee, the Committee against Torture, the Committee on Economic, Social and Cultural Rights, the Committee on the Protection of the Rights of All Migrant Workers and Members of their Families (which held its first session in March 2004) and the Committee on the Rights of the Child.

[11] Ph. Alston, 'Appraising the United Nations Human Rights Regime', *l.c.* (note 6), pp. 3–5.

[12] Except for the International Court of Justice, which is a judicial organ.

[13] The reporting procedure is laid down in Article 40 of the CCPR, Articles 16–17 of the CESCR, Article 9 of the CERD, Article 18 of the CEDAW, Article 19 of the CAT, Article 44 of the CRC and in Article 73 of the CMW.

[14] See for example Articles 41–42 of the CCPR, Articles 11–13 of the CERD, Article 21 of the CAT, and Article 76 of the MWC. Within the framework of the UN, the term 'communications' is rather used than 'complaints'. Opsahl describes the term 'communications' as a UN-euphemism for 'complaints': T. Opsahl, 'The Human Rights Committee', in: Ph. Alston (ed.), *The United Nations and Human Rights. A Critical Appraisal* (Oxford, Clarendon Press, 1992), p. 419; see also M. Bossuyt, 'De werking van het VN – Comité Mensenrechten', in: Interuniversitair Centrum Mensenrechten (ed.), *De betekenis van het Internationaal Verdrag inzake Burgerrechten en Politieke Rechten voor de interne rechtsorde* (Antwerp/Apeldoorn, Maklu, 1993), p. 10.

[15] See for example the first Optional Protocol to the CCPR, the Optional Protocol to the CEDAW, Article 14 of the CERD, Article 22 of the CAT, and Article 77 of the MWC. See also the draft Optional Protocol to the CESCR, which is still under consideration.

[16] The intention of country procedures is to thoroughly examine flagrant violations of human rights in a certain country. This can be realized by delegating special rapporteurs or individual experts to the country concerned or by founding a working group. See http://www.unhchr.ch/html/menu2/7/a/cm.htm.

procedures[17] and confidential procedures (*e.g.* procedure 1503).[18] The intention of all these procedures is to check and encourage the implementation of human rights by the States and not to judicially enforce human rights.[19] The first three procedures are used by 'treaty-based organs', the latter three are the instruments of the 'charter-based organs'. The procedure before the CRC Committee is a reporting procedure.

---

[17] Thematic procedures are applied to examine the violation of certain human rights (such as torture, religious intolerance etc.). They include special rapporteurs dealing with the sale of children, child prostitution and child pornography; the right to the enjoyment of the highest attainable standard of physical and mental health; the right to education; extra judicial, summary and arbitrary executions, the right to food etc. They further include individual experts dealing with the right to development, the protection of persons from enforced or involuntary disappearance, etc. They also include working groups on arbitrary detention, on enforced and involuntary internally displaced persons and on problems of racial discrimination faced by people of African descent etc. See http://www.unhchr.ch/ html/menu2/ 7/b/tm.htm.

[18] Procedure 1503 was established in 1970 by the Economic and Social Council and amended during the fifty-sixth session of the Commission on Human Rights in 2000. See http://www.unhchr.ch/html/menu2/8/1503.htm.

[19] Procedures through which judgements by an international court can be imposed on the violating State are less developed within the UN. Parmentier states that only the procedure for the International Court of Justice matches this description to a certain degree: S. Parmentier, 'Internationale controle en implementatie van mensenrechten', in: *Belgen over mensenrechten – Een bijdrage tot de Wereldconferentie Mensenrechten, Vienna, 14-25 June 1993* (Brussels, Belgian Ministry of Foreign Affairs, Foreign Trade and Development Cooperation, 1993), p. 28. One can also assume that the respective *ad hoc* International Tribunals established to review events that have taken place in the former Yugoslavia and in Rwanda, and the permanent International Criminal Court, match, at least to a certain extent, the same description. This category is more extended at a regional level. The European Court of Human Rights is for example qualified to pronounce judgements which are legally binding for the States that have ratified the European Convention on Human Rights. A person who cannot enforce his rights before a national judge can hence appeal to an international judge.

CHAPTER THREE

THE STRUCTURE OF THE CRC COMMITTEE

1. *The Birth of the CRC Committee*

6. By virtue of Article 43(1) of the Convention, the CRC Committee was installed to assess the progress made by the States regarding the fulfilment of their obligations.

7. The *Travaux Préparatoires* of the Convention show that not every country gave its downright approval to develop a separate Committee on children's rights. A lot of countries were aware of the problems that are implied by an increase in the number of control organs within the United Nations, such as financial implications,[20] problems due to vagueness and overlaps, strains put on national administrations etc. It was the Belgian delegate who suggested leaving the monitoring of the implementation of the CRC to the existing Committees. He more specifically meant the monitoring organs of the two Covenants of 1966.[21] Poland suggested to have the reports examined by a 'Group of Governmental Experts', founded by the Economic and Social Council.[22] However, neither proposal was adopted. Instead, the foundation of a separate Committee on children's rights was finally opted for. The argument that no UN-body has an overall view on the rights of the child has had a decisive influence on the discussion.[23] Hence, the CRC Committee

---

[20] In the course of *the Travaux Préparatoires*, a lot of attention was paid to the financial implications of the increase in the number of committees: S. Detrick (ed.), *The United Nations Convention on the Rights of the Child: A Guide to the "Travaux Préparatoires"* (Dordrecht, Boston, London, Martinus Nijhoff Publishers, 1992), p. 555 et seq.

[21] *Ibid.*, p. 555.

[22] The Polish proposal was formulated as follows: '1. Reports submitted by the States Parties to the present Convention under Article 22 shall be considered by the Economic and Social Council, which may bring its observations and suggestions to the attention of the State Party concerned and of the General Assembly of the United Nations. The Council may also request a State Party to submit additional reports on specific issues relating to this Convention. To assist it in its task, the Economic and Social Council shall establish a Group of Governmental Experts entrusted with the responsibility of examining the reports submitted by States Parties. . . .': S. Detrick (ed.), *The United Nations Convention on the Rights of the Child: A Guide to the "Travaux Préparatoires"*, *o.c.* (note 20), p. 552.

[23] 'One representative expressed her belief that neither in the United Nations system nor among the non-governmental international organisations was there at present a legal entity which had an overall view of the rights of the child: it therefore believed that if it proved

interpretations and hence jeopardize a coherent interpretation of the Convention. However, the split would not have to be permanent. According to the president of the Committee, five sessions would suffice to eliminate the backlog.[36] The Committee hence has asked the Secretary-General to supply funding for two years and will after an evaluation of this working method decide whether it will continue this process. In December 2004, the General Assembly approved the proposed working method and its financial implications. From 2005 onwards, the Committee will therefore work in two chambers, for a period of two years, in order to clear the backlog.[37]

10. The Committee members act independently, *i.e.* in their own capacity without being accountable to their governments.[38] The Committee wants to keep this notion of independence high and therefore it has decided that its members will not participate in the discussion on the country report of their own government.[39]

11. Article 43 provides a specific procedure for the election of the Committee members.[40] They are elected by the States Parties for a period of four years.[41] However, the Committee can have a different composition every two years as the term of office of five of the members[42] who were elected during the first elections[43] came to an end after two years. The members are eligible

[36] UN Doc. CRC/C/SR.858, 2003, para. 39.

[37] CRC Committee, *Recommendation on its Working Methods* (UN Doc. CRC/C/133, 2004), pp. 4–5. See also UN Docs. A/59/499, para. 26, A/C.3/59/L.82/Add.1., A/C.3/59/L.29/Rev.1, para. 9 and CRC/C/143, 2005, Annex III, pp. 122–123.

[38] Article 43(2) of the CRC.

[39] UN Doc. CRC/C/10, 1992, para. 33; Van Bueren points at the relativity of this notion: 'The notion of independence, however, has to be considered with some caution. It is unlikely that a State Party will nominate any candidate who publicly disagrees with the policies of the government of the day': see G. Van Bueren, *o.c.* (note 5), p. 384.

[40] See Article 43(3), (4), (5), (6) and (7) of the CRC. The procedure can roughly be outlined as follows: 1° Each State Party of the Convention may nominate one person from among its own nationals. The Secretary-General of the United Nations invites the States Parties to submit their nominations within a period of two months. He is to do so at least four months before the elections actually take place; 2° The Secretary-General draws up an alphabetical list of all nominated persons, mentioning the countries they were nominated by. This list will then be submitted to the States Parties of the Convention; 3° The elections are held at a meeting organised by the Secretary-General. All States Parties are invited to this meeting. At least two thirds of the States Parties must attend the meeting. To be elected, a candidate must obtain an absolute majority of the votes of the attending delegates of voting States. Those who have the most votes are elected.

[41] See also CRC Committee, *the Provisional Rules of Procedure* (UN Doc. CRC/C/4, 1991), Rule 12.

[42] These five members were appointed by the President of the Meeting by means of a lottery.

[43] The first election of the Committee members took place between the 27th of February and the 1st of March 1991: see UN Doc. CRC/C/7, para. 3.

for re-election if they are re-nominated.[44] Consideration is given to equitable geographical distribution and to the principal legal systems.[45] From among its members, the Committee elects officers for a term of two years.[46] These include one Chairperson, three Vice-Chairpersons and one Rapporteur.[47]

3. The Official and Informal Meetings of the CRC Committee

12. The CRC Committee held its first session in 1991 at the UN Headquarters in Geneva.[48] The Committee's firsts sessions (in both 1991 and 1992) were devoted to practical matters, such as the drafting of its Provisional Rules of Procedure[49] and the reporting guidelines. It was not until 1993 that the Committee began to examine States Parties' reports.

The Convention itself requires that the Committee meets annually,[50] which it initially did. However, during its first session, the Committee already noted that one session a year would not do to meet its objectives.[51] This is why the Committee deemed it necessary to ask the General Assembly to authorise the Secretary-General to organise at least two sessions a year. Moreover, the Committee asked the General Assembly's permission to found a 'pre-sessional working group'.[52] The latter has approved both demands in resolution 46/112.[53] Nevertheless, the main problem of the Committee remained the lack of time. Indeed, the CRC had, in a very short period,

---

[44] Article 43(6) of the CRC.
[45] Article 43(2) of the CRC.
[46] Article 43(9) of the CRC.
[47] CRC Committee, *the Provisional Rules of Procedure* (UN Doc. CRC/C/4, 1991), Rules 16–17. From the moment the Committee will consist of two chambers (*Cf. supra* No 9), two rapporteurs will be appointed, one for each chamber.
[48] Article 43(10) of the CRC states that the normal meeting place for the Committee is at the UN Headquarters but grants the Committee the liberty to meet at 'any other convenient place'. See also CRC Committee, *the Provisional Rules of Procedure* (UN Doc. CRC/C/4, 1991), Rule 4.
[49] See CRC Committee, *the Provisional Rules of Procedure* (UN Doc. CRC/C/4, 1991), drafted in accordance with Article 43(8) of the CRC. The Rules of procedure deal with issues such as the working process, the drafting of the agenda, the duties of the Secretariat, the official and working languages, functions such as holding sessions, electing the officers, and distributing reports. Also the functions of the Committee are addressed, including the examination of the reports, the drafting of general comments and the organisation of general days of discussion.
[50] Article 43(10) of the CRC.
[51] UN Doc. CRC/C/7, 1991, p. 10, para. 5.
[52] CRC Committee, *Conclusions and Recommendations adopted on the sessions of the Committee or its subsidiary bodies* (UN Doc. CRC/C/7, 1991), p. 3.
[53] UN Doc. A/RES/46/112, 1992.

become the UN Convention with the largest number of ratifications.[54] It was in the course of its fourth session (1993) that the Committee decided to organise a special session in 1994.[55] At the fifth session (1994), the Secretary-General was asked to organise a meeting of the States Parties at which the duration of the meetings would be discussed. He was at the same time asked to increase the number of both the annual sessions and of the meetings of the 'Pre-sessional Working Group' from two to three.[56] Since 1995, the Committee holds three sessions a year. Each session comprises a three-week period[57] and is followed by an additional week for the pre-sessional working group.

13. Apart from the official sessions, the Committee has organised a number of informal regional meetings.[58] These meetings intend to promote the provisions of the CRC on a regional level, to encourage international cooperation in the field of children's rights and to offer its members the opportunity to examine the situation of the rights of the child on the spot.[59] The CRC Committee was the first UN treaty body to study the situation of

---

[54] Somalia and the United States of America are the only countries that have not ratified the Convention.

[55] CRC Committee, *Conclusions and Recommendations adopted on the organisation of work — sessions of the Committee and its subsidiary bodies* (UN Doc. CCR/C/20, 1993), p. 4.

[56] CRC Committee, *Conclusions and Recommendations adopted on the organisation of work — sessions of the Committee and its subsidiary bodies* (UN Doc. CRC/C/24, 1994), p. 4.

[57] The duration of the sessions is determined by a meeting of the States Parties of the Convention, subject to the approval of the General Assembly (Article 43(10) of the CRC).

[58] The first meeting was held in Quito, Ecuador between the 1st and the 5th of June 1992. The meeting was organised and financed by UNICEF and the Human Rights Centre : see UN Doc. CRC/C/10, 1992, p. 1. The second meeting took place in Bangkok, Thailand, between the 23rd and the 29th of May 1993 : see UN Doc. CRC/C/20, 1993, paras. 143–149. The third meeting took place in Africa, between the 11th and the 22e of July 1994: see UN Doc. CRC/C/34, 1994, paras. 156–159. The fourth informal meeting took place for two weeks in October 1995 in the South Asian region: see UN Doc. CRC/C/46, 1995, paras. 186–194. The fifth informal meeting took place for two weeks in November 1996 in the Northern African region: see UN Doc. CRC/C/62, 1997, paras. 248–259. It is important to note that the visit to Egypt was the occasion of the holding, for the first time, of joint meetings between the CRC Committee and the CEDAW Committee. It was agreed that the meetings had contributed to establishing a framework for more interaction between the two Committees and it was decided to follow up with periodic meetings to ensure further collaboration in the future on a regular basis: see UN Doc. CRC/C/62, 1997, para. 257. From 29 May to 1 June 1998, the Committee was invited by the Italian authorities, with the support of the Italian National Committee for UNICEF, for an informal visit to Florence: see UN Doc. CRC/C/79, 1998, para. 294. On 27 and 28 May 2000, the Committee undertook another informal visit to Italy in which the educational system was focused upon: see UN Doc. CRC/C/97, 2000, para. 597.

[59] UN Docs. CRC/C/10, 1992, p. 14, para. 34 and CRC/C/20, 1993, para. 143.

[60] UN Doc. CRC/C/SR.29, 1992, para. 7.

human rights on the spot in certain countries.[60] [61] The Committee does however stress the fact that the regional informal meetings have no control function at all. They are merely considered as an educational and training exercise.[62] By means of listening to children on the spot the Committee has given shape to one of the most important reasons of the Convention's existence: the participation of the children themselves.[63]

Besides these informal regional visits, the Committee sometimes holds informal meetings with the States Parties tot the CRC. During these meetings, issues such as the reporting process, the implications of the increase of the membership of the Committee, and the Secretary-General's proposals to reform the UN treaty body system are the subjects of an interactive dialogue.[64]

Furthermore, the Committee members often take part in conferences, seminars, courses and other meetings concerning children's rights issues. These so-called 'intersessional activities' contribute to the visibility of the CRC and its Committee and hence to a better realisation of the rights of the child.

---

[61] It was during the second session (1992) that the Committee decided to call the attention of the 'Fourth Meeting of persons chairing the human rights treaty bodies' to this work method: 'The innovating experience of holding informal meetings at the regional level should be brought to the attention of the Fourth Meeting, in view of its relevance as a means to promote greater awareness of the Convention on the Rights of the Child and its system of implementation, and to provide the Committee with a deeper knowledge and better understanding of the realities of a region'; see CRC Committee, *Conclusions and Recommendations adopted on the Fourth Meeting of persons chairing the human rights treaty bodies* (UN Doc. CRC/C/10, 1992), pp. 5–6.

[62] UN Doc. CRC/C/SR.29, 1992, para. 14.

[63] R. Reid, 'Children's Rights: Radical Remedies for Critical Needs', in: S. Asquith, and M. Hill (eds.) *Justice for Children* (Dordrecht/Boston/London, Martinus Nijhoff Publishers, 1994), p. 21.

[64] *E.g.* UN Docs. CRC/C/124, 2003, para. 509; and CRC/C/137, 2004, para. 668.

CHAPTER FOUR

THE ACTIONS OF THE CRC COMMITTEE

14. The functions to be performed by the CRC Committee are outlined in Articles 44 and 45 of the CRC. The Committee has two main tasks: firstly, examining the progress made by the States in giving effect to the convention's standards and secondly, assisting and advising the States in implementing the Convention. These functions are chiefly performed through the reporting procedure.

1. *The Reporting Procedure*

1.1 *The Content of the Reports*

15. A first step in the reporting procedure is the submission of the reports by the States Parties. In accordance with Article 44(1) of the CRC, the States 'undertake to submit to the Committee (. . .) reports on the measures they have adopted which give effect to the rights recognized herein and on the progress made on the enjoyment of those rights'. The words 'undertake to submit' make clear that the reporting procedure is mandatory to the States Parties.[65] They are under an obligation to regularly draw up reports and to address them to the Secretary-General, who communicates them to the Committee. The States also have an obligation to make sure that their reports are publicly available in their own country.[66]

16. An obvious condition for this monitoring system to be effective is that the States Parties take their reporting obligation seriously. Firstly, a State should respect the deadlines, being initially two years after the Convention entered into force for it and subsequently every five years.[67] The same

---

[65] Contrary to the individual and inter – state communications procedures under other UN treaties, which are generally optional (except for the mandatory inter-state communications procedure under Articles 11–13 of the CERD).

[66] Article 44(6) of the CRC.

[67] Article 44(1) of the CRC. The Committee started its consideration of periodic reports as from its nineteenth session in September-October 1998. As of 1 October 2004, the Committee has received 281 reports, 182 initial ones, 87 periodic ones and 12 third periodic ones: see UN Doc. CRC/C/142, 2004, para. 3.

deadlines count for the reporting obligation to the Optional Protocols to the Convention.[68] Secondly, the governments should submit a report of good quality. The report must provide the amount and kind of information the Committee needs in order to fulfil its monitoring task. It may thus not be incomplete and superficial. In this regard the Convention itself (Article 44) stays rather vague. Hence, the Committee has adopted several sets of reporting guidelines in order to guide the States Parties in drafting their reports.

1.1.1   Article 44 of the CRC

17. According to Article 44, the reports should contain the following: Firstly, the States should list the measures they have adopted which give effect to the rights recognised in the Convention. At the same time they also have to give information on the progress made on the real enjoyment of those rights.[69] This means that the States are obliged to assess the effect of the measures they took. They have to check whether those have contributed to the realisation of the rights of the child. Secondly, the same Article specifies that the reports are to mention the 'factors and the possible difficulties' that have their influence on the compliance with the obligations entailed by the Convention.[70] States that, in one way or another, experience some difficulties with the implementation of the Convention, have the opportunity to communicate these difficulties to the Committee. The Committee can then give its advice on the matter concerned. Finally, Article 44 mentions that the reports are to contain sufficient information in order to provide the Committee with a comprehensive understanding of the implementation of the Convention in the country concerned.[71] The Committee can always request more information from a State if the report does not allow it to acquire such a comprehensive impression.[72] In order not to burden the States too much, it is also stipulated that a State, which has submitted a comprehensive initial report to the Committee does not need to repeat basic information previously provided in its subsequent reports.[73]

18. It should be admitted that the reporting obligations under Article 44 of the CRC are wider and more general than those under the 'older' treaties.

---

[68] Article 8 of the Optional Protocol on the involvement of children in armed conflict and Article 12 of Optional Protocol on the sale of children, child prostitution and child pornography.
[69] Article 44(1) of the CRC.
[70] Article 44(2) of the CRC.
[71] Article 44(2) of the CRC.
[72] Article 44(4) of the CRC.
[73] Article 44(3) of the CRC.

The CERD for instance, only requires that the States Parties 'undertake to submit (...) a report on the legislative, judicial, administrative or other measures which they have adopted and which give effect tot the provisions of this Convention'.[74] The CEDAW adds that 'reports *may* indicate factors and difficulties affecting the degree of fulfilment of obligations'.[75] The CCPR goes yet a step further by requiring that the reports '*shall* indicate the factors and difficulties' but leaves out the important CRC provision which obliges the States to supply 'sufficient information to provide the Committee with *a comprehensive understanding of the implementation of the Convention in the Country concerned*'.[76] As Dimitrijevic argues, this more rigorous process of reporting contained in the CRC is 'due to the experiences gathered in the course of the examination of reports by treaty bodies, which indicated that a meaningful study and evaluation of reports necessitated not only information about measures that have the nature of legal acts (acts of state), but a deeper understanding of the wider conditions in the whole society ('facts and difficulties', 'comprehensive understanding of the situation')'.[77]

Notwithstanding the advanced nature of Article 44 of the CRC –as compared to the equivalent articles in other UN treaties–, the stipulations in Article 44 still leave the governments with a lot of questions: how are the reports to be drawn up? How exhaustive and specific should the reports be? How is it to be checked whether progress has been made relating to the enjoyment of human rights? When is the information considered to be 'sufficient' as implied by Article 44(2)? These are answered in the several sets of reporting guidelines, the CRC Committee drew up and which are outlined below.

1.1.2 *The Reporting Guidelines*
19. The CRC Committee adopted a first set of guidelines on 15 October 1991. These guidelines should be followed by a State Party when drawing up its initial report.[78] A second set of guidelines was adopted in 1996, for the drawing up of the periodic reports.[79] Yet another set of guidelines, *i.e.* the so-called 'consolidated guidelines', exist for the introductory part of

[74] Article 9(1) of the CERD.
[75] Article 18(2) of the CEDAW (emphasis added).
[76] Emphasis added.
[77] V. Dimitrijevic, 'State Reports', in: G. Alfredsson, J. Grimheden, B.G. Ramcharan and A. de Zayas (eds.), *International Human Rights Monitoring Mechanisms. Essays in Honour of Jakob Th. Möller* (The Hague/Boston/London, Martinus Nijhoff Publishers, 2001), p. 191.
[78] CRC Committee, *General guidelines regarding the form and content of initial reports to be submitted by States Parties under Article 44, paragraph 1(a), of the Convention* (UN Docs. CRC/C/5, 1991 and CRC/C/7, 1991, Annex III).
[79] CRC Committee, *General Guidelines regarding the form and the contents of the periodic reports* (UN Doc. CRC/C/58, 1996).

the report.[80] Reporting guidelines are not binding on the States Parties but rather give an expression to certain expectations of the Committee and should avoid that the Committee has to request additional information.[81]

20. In the introductory part, the States have to inform the Committee about the population and the general institutional and judicial framework of the country. The description of this institutional framework may be the same for each report that has to be submitted to one of the UN treaty-based organs.[82]

21. The guidelines of 1991 provide indications on the nature and depth of the information required and also impose some uniform structure on the production of the initial reports. The guidelines group the articles of the CRC into eight broad themes, which are the headings of the prescribed structure of the report. This classification entails that the articles of the Convention are grouped per topic instead of the more usual article-by-article approach. The thematic approach stresses the interrelationship between the Convention's articles better and encourages the holistic approach to implementation.[83]

The eight sections of the report are listed below:

(1) *General measures of implementation*: this section should contain the description of the measures taken by the States to harmonise national law and policy with the provisions of the Convention. At the same time, all mechanisms that have been or that will be established on a national or a local level for co-ordinating policies relating to children and for monitoring the implementation of the Convention are to be described. The way in which the report will be made public in the country concerned and the way in which the population (adults and children) will be informed of the provisions of the Convention are to be mentioned as well.

(2) *Definition of the child*: the States have to inform the Committee about how the word 'child' (Article 1 of the CRC) is defined in their legislation. The report must especially indicate the age when majority is attained and the minimum age for such purposes as marriage, sexual consent, end of compulsory education, legal counselling without parental consent etc.

---

[80] UN Doc. HRI/CORE/1, 1992, Annex. See also X., *Manuel relatif à l'établissement des rapports sur les droits de l'homme* (New York, Nations Unies, 1992), pp. 33–34.

[81] M. Nowak, *U.N. Covenant on Civil and Political Rights—CCPR Commentary* (Kehl/Strasbourg/Arlington, N.P. Engel Publisher, 1993), p. 558.

[82] UN Doc. HRI/CORE/1, 1992, Annex. See also X., *Manuel relatif à l'établissement des rapports sur les droits de l'homme* (New York, Nations Unies, 1992), pp. 33–34.

[83] J. Karp, 'Reporting and the Committee on the Rights of the Child', in: A.F. Bayefsky (ed.), *The UN Human Rights System in the 21st Century* (The Hague/London/Boston, Kluwer Law International, 2000), pp. 36–38.

(3) *General principles*: The Committee identifies four underlying principles in the Convention, which are considered as essential, *i.e.* as if they were incorporated in each other provision of the Convention: the non-discrimination principle (Article 2), the best interest of the child (Article 3), the right to life, survival and development (Article 6) and respect for the views of the child (Article 12). The States Parties are to give information regarding these principles and are to include in this part of their reports information on the application of these principles in the implementation of articles cited in other sections of the guidelines.

(4) *Civil rights and freedoms*: under this heading information must be provided on the civil rights and freedoms enshrined in the Convention.[84]

(5) *Family environment and alternative care*: the rights of the child in relation to his or her family are to be described in this section.[85]

(6) *Basic health and welfare*: this heading contains information on a number of social and economic rights of the Convention, such as health care services etc.[86]

(7) A seventh heading contains information on *Education, leisure and cultural activities*.[87]

(8) *Special protection measures*: this section is split up into four sub-sections, being 1) children in situations of emergency;[88] 2) children in conflict with the law;[89] 3) children in situations of exploitation (including physical and

---

[84] More specifically: name and nationality (Article 7), preservation of identity (Article 8), freedom of expression (Article 13), access to appropriate information (Article 17), freedom of thought, conscience and religion (Article 14), freedom of association and of peaceful assembly (Article 15), protection of privacy (Article 16) and the right not to be subjected to torture or other cruel, inhuman or degrading treatment or punishment (Article 37(a)).

[85] More specifically: parental guidance (Article 5), parental responsibilities (Article 18(1) and (2)), separation from parents (Article 9), family reunification (Article 10), recovery of maintenance for the child (Article 27(4)), children deprived of a family environment (Article 20), adoption (Article 21), illicit transfer and non-return (Article 11), abuse and neglect, including physical and psychological recovery and social reintegration (Article 19), periodic review of placement (Article 25) and physical and psychological recovery and social integration (Article 39). The States must also supply the Committee with the necessary information on the way in which the 'best interest of the child' and the opinion of the child are being taken into account.

[86] More specifically: survival and development (Article 6(2)), disabled children (Article 23), health and health services (Article 24), social security and child care services and facilities (Articles 26 and 18(3)) and standard of living (Article 27(1) to (3)). Within this framework, the States should describe a/o the infrastructure of their health care policy.

[87] More specifically: vocational training and guidance (Article 28), aims of education (Article 29) and leisure, recreation and cultural activities (Article 31). The Committee asks the States to supply some information on the provided infrastructure when carrying out their policies regarding education.

[88] More specifically: Refugee children (Article 22), children in armed conflicts (Article 38) and physical and psychological recovery and social reintegration (Article 39).

[89] More specifically: The administration of justice (Article 40), children deprived of liberty including imprisonment, detention or placement in custodial settings (Article 37) and sentencing of juveniles (Article 37).

psychological recovery and social reintegration)[90] and 4) children belonging to a minority or an indigenous group.[91]

22. In its initial guidelines, the Committee emphasises the importance of effective national implementation measures. In section 1, States are asked to describe the mechanisms at national or local level for coordinating policies relating to children and for monitoring the implementation of the Convention. Sections 6 (basic health and welfare) and 7 (education, leisure and cultural activities) also mention a similar monitoring mechanism. Also the concluding observations to the States Parties' reports show that the Committee sets great store by a national follow-up structure of this kind. The States are either congratulated with the existence of a national follow-up structure, or they are urged to establish one.[92] The Committee recommended *inter alia* the establishment of inter-ministerial committees, interdepartmental cooperation, child impact statements, annual reports to the parliament, dialogue with NGOs etc. These recommendations have led to initiatives in many countries. Furthermore, in 2002 the Committee adopted a general comment on the role of independent national human rights institutions in the promotion and protection of children's rights.[93] It considers the establishment of such bodies to fall within the commitment made by the States Parties under Article 4, *i.e.* to ensure the implementation of the Convention. The emphasis on the monitoring of children's rights at the national level confirms the recognition that the reporting procedure is to strengthen the national capacity to monitor children's rights. The Convention itself does not explicitly mention a national monitoring and coordinating mechanism.

23. The value of these guidelines and more specifically of the thematic approach lies in the fact that the Committee receives better-structured reports. It also facilitates the participation of specialised agencies and NGOs that are well-skilled in certain aspects of the CRC.[94] However, the Committee

---

[90] More specifically: economic exploitation (Article 32), drug abuse (Article 33), sexual exploitation and abuse (Article 34), sale, trafficking and abduction (Article 35) and other forms of exploitation (Article 36).

[91] Article 30 of the CRC.

[92] *E.g.* CRC Committee, *Concluding Observations: Bolivia* (UN Doc. CRC/C/16, 1993), para. 29; *the Russian Federation* (UN Doc. CRC/C/16, 1993), *Sudan* (UN Doc. CRC/C/20, 1993), para. 110 ; *Denmark* (UN Doc. CRC/C/38, 1995), para. 173; *Belgium* (UN Doc. CRC/C/43, 1995), para. 103; *Burundi* (UN Doc. CRC/C/100, 2000), paras. 97–98; and *Armenia* (UN Doc. CRC/C/137, 2004), paras. 186–187.

[93] CRC Committee, *General Comment No 2 (2002), The role of independent national human rights institutions in the promotion and protection of the rights of the child* (UN Doc. CRC/GC/2002/2, 2002).

[94] D. Goodman, 'Analysis of the first session of the Committee on the Rights of the Child', *Netherlands Quarterly of Human Rights* 1, 1992, p. 50.

did stress that this classification is not a classification based on the importance of the rights. All rights remain equally important.

On the other hand, some shortcomings were detected in the first set of guidelines. Abramson states: 'One glaring inadequacy of the guidelines is that they do not ask States for any information on spending. Even the most elementary questions about what percentage of the budget goes to children's health or education are omitted. States merely 'are encouraged' to provide relevant statistical information and indicators. The State is given total freedom to decide what is relevant'.[95] This situation has led to a large diversity in the quality of the reports.[96] Some of them met the quality standards. However, others turned out to contain insufficient information.[97] When the country reports lack the most elementary information – such as the percentages of the Gross National Product that go to children's health care or education – the Committee cannot but spend most of the meeting on the gathering of additional information and little time remains to hold a debate. The quality of the reports thus determines the quality of the debate between the Committee and the government representatives. Nevertheless, the gaps in the guidelines are quite understandable. At the time when they were drawn up, the Committee did not have a clear view on what the reports and the 'constructive dialogue' would lead to. It was obvious that the Committee still had to draw the necessary and useful lessons from the initial reports of the countries.

24. In drafting its second set of guidelines in 1996,[98] the Committee took the above mentioned shortcomings into consideration. These guidelines were produced for the periodic reports. They request the States Parties to maintain the above mentioned eight headings. At the same time they require a

---

[95] B. Abramson, 'First State reports: Sunny and … cloudy', *International children's rights monitor* 10, No. 1–2, 1993, p. 23; See also: D. Goodman, *l.c.* (note 94), p. 51; J.R. Himes, 'Reflecting on indicators concerning the rights of the child – The development and human rights communities should get their acts together', in: *Innocenti essays No 5. The United Nations Convention on the Rights of the Child: Three Essays on the Challenge of Implementation* (Unicef, Florence, 1993), p. 20; J. Smith, 'The Committee on the Rights of the Child', *Netherlands Quarterly of Human Rights*, 1994, p. 322; L. Theytaz-Bergman, 'Adjustments urgently needed. Fourth session of the Committee on the Rights of the Child', *International children's rights monitor* 10, No 4, 1993, p. 22.

[96] On the first reports, see: B. Abramson, 'First State reports: Sunny and … cloudy', *l.c.* (note 95), pp. 22–37.

[97] *E.g.* CRC Committee, *Concluding Observations: Rwanda* (UN Doc. CRC/C/20, 1993), para. 139; *Sudan* (UN Doc. CRC/C/16, 1993) para. 111; *Peru* (UN Doc. CRC/C/20, 1993), para. 56; and *Indonesia* (UN Doc. CRC/C/20, 1993), para. 37.

[98] During its tenth session, the Committee decided to establish a working group with a view to preparing a working paper on the conceptual framework for guidelines regarding the form and content of the periodic reports: see UN Doc. CRC/C/46, 1995, para. 241. During

more rigorous process of reporting from the governments.[99] They distinguish themselves from the initial guidelines, firstly, by containing more detailed questions regarding *inter alia* the proportion of the budget devoted to social expenditures for children (health, education, welfare, etc.), the budget trend over the period covered by the report, the steps taken to ensure that the authorities are guided by the best interests of the child in their budgetary decisions etc.; secondly, by stressing the importance of the follow-up of the Committee's recommendations[100] and thirdly by emphasizing the importance of the establishment of implementation strategies, the importance of data and information collection and of the development of appropriate indicators not only to measure the achievement in the realisation of the rights but also to measure the violation of rights.[101]

These guidelines thus ask for more detailed information than the first set. On the one hand, this was a necessary response to the shortcomings of the first set, but, on the other hand, it had the unfortunate side effect of leading to overly lengthy reports. In reaction and taking into account its own workload, the Committee formulated in 2002 a recommendation in which it proclaimed a review of the guidelines for periodic reporting in the near future. In the same recommendation the Committee asked the States to limit their reports to 120 pages and to focus on key implementation issues, such as fundamental developments in the period since the last report

---

its eleventh session, the Committee decided to establish a working group to prepare a draft document for that purpose: see UN Docs. CRC/C/50, 1996, para. 245. The guidelines were adopted by the Committee at its 343rd meeting: see UN Doc. CRC/C/57, 1996, para. 222; for the text of the guidelines, see CRC Committee, *General Guidelines regarding the form and the contents of the periodic reports* (UN Doc. CRC/C/58, 1996).

[99] *E.g.* under the heading 'General measures of implementation' the States are asked to give information about (1) the steps undertaken to ensure coordination between economic and social policies; (2) the proportion of the budget devoted to social expenditures for children, including health, welfare and education, at the central, regional and local levels, and where appropriate at the federal and provincial levels; (3) the budget trends over the period covered by the report; (4) arrangements for budgetary analysis enabling the amount and proportion spent on children to be clearly identified; (5) the steps taken to ensure that all competent national, regional and local authorities are guided by the best interests of the child in their budgetary decisions and evaluate the priority given to children in their policy-making; (6) the measures taken to ensure that disparities between different regions and groups of children are bridged in relation to the provision of social services; and (7) the measures taken to ensure that children, particularly those belonging to the most disadvantaged groups, are protected against the adverse effects of economic policies, including the reduction of budgetary allocations in the social sector. CRC Committee, *General Guidelines regarding the form and the contents of the periodic reports* (UN Doc. CRC/C/58, 1996), para. 20.

[100] In the first part of each periodic report, the government has to respond to the suggestions and recommendations the Committee made in its previous concluding observations.

[101] UN docs. CRC/C/57, 1996, para. 222 and CRC/C/58, 1996 paras. 18 and 20.

and measures taken to implement the Committee's concluding observations. The Committee further urged the States not to repeat information already contained in previous reports. They finally were recommended to include information not only on the situation *de jure* but also on the situation *de facto*.[102]

25. Since the entering into force of the two optional protocols to the Convention in 2002,[103] the States Parties to these protocols are obliged to submit their first reports providing comprehensive information on the measures they have taken to implement the provisions of these protocols.[104] To this purpose, the Committee drafted separate guidelines for each protocol.[105]

1.2   The Study of the Reports by the CRC Committee

26. The reports are considered in three steps which are outlined below.

1.2.1   The Pre-sessional Working Group

27. In a first stage, the reports are reviewed by a pre-sessional working group. This working group normally meets for one week immediately after a plenary session of the Committee, in a closed meeting, to prepare for the next session. The working group consists of the Committee members.[106]

---

[102] CRC Committee, *Recommendation on the Organization of Work* (UN Doc. CRC/C/118, 2002), pp. 4–5.

[103] *Cf. supra* note 1.

[104] In September 2003, the Committee considered for the first time a report under one of the optional protocols: New Zealand entered into dialogue with the Committee regarding the efforts it had made to implement the Optional Protocol on the involvement of children in armed conflicts: see UN Doc. CRC/C/133, 2004, paras. 589–600. For reporting under the Optional Protocol on the involvement of children in armed conflict, see T. Vandewiele, 'Optional Protocol to the Covention on the Rights of the Child: The involment of Children in Armed Conflicts', in: A. Alen, J. Vande Lanotte, E. Verhellen, F. Ang, E. Berghmans and M. Verheyde (eds.), *A Commentary on the United Nations Convention on the Rights of the Child* (Leiden/Boston, Martinus Nijhoff Publishers, 2005), pp. 58–62. For reporting under the Optional Protocol on the sale of children, child prostitution and child pornography, see J.M. Petit, 'Optional Protocol to the Convention of the Rights of the Child on the Sale of Children, Child Prostitution and Child Pornography', in: A. Alen, J. Vande Lanotte, E. Verhellen, F. Ang, E. Berghmans and M. Verheyde (eds.), *A Commentary on the United Nations Convention on the Rights of the Child* (Leiden/Boston, Martinus Nijhoff Publishers, 2005).

[105] CRC Committee, *Guidelines regarding initial reports to be submitted by States Parties to the Optional Protocol to the Convention on the Rights of the Child on the involvement of children in armed conflict* (UN Doc. CRC/OP/AC/1, 2001) and CRC Committee, *Guidelines regarding initial reports to be submitted by States Parties under Article 12, paragraph 1, of the Optional Protocol to the Convention on the Rights of the Child on the Sale of children, child prostitution and child pornography* (UN Doc. CRC/OP/SA/1, 2002).

[106] All Committee members are invited to the pre-sessional working group.

Representatives of the UN bodies and agencies can take part in the meeting.[107] The working group can also invite representatives of NGOs. Government representatives and observers, on the other hand, are not allowed to attend.

28. The principal purpose of the working group is to facilitate the Committee's work under Articles 44 and 45 of the Convention, primarily by reviewing State Party reports and identifying in advance the main questions that should be discussed with the representatives of the reporting States.[108] It also provides an opportunity to consider questions relating to technical assistance and international cooperation. The resulting questionnaire ('list of issues') is sent to the State in order to enable the representative to prepare himself for the Committee's dialogue.

29. An advantage of this way of proceeding is that it reduces the possibility that the representative would make no reply to the questions. Another advantage is that NGOs and individual experts can be efficiently involved in the monitoring process.[109] The Committee has adopted guidelines to facilitate and encourage the process of written submission of NGO reports

---

[107] There is a particular interest in receiving relevant information from certain bodies like ILO, UNICEF, WHO and World Bank.

[108] In this task, the pre-sessional working group is assisted by the Committee Secretariat. The staff members of the Secretariat do the preliminary analysis of the reports, prepare substantive background papers, draw up a draft list of issues which is afterwards submitted to the working group for adoption.

[109] See UN Doc. CRC/C/38, 1995, paras. 262–263: 'Non-governmental organizations may (. . .) provide expert advice to the Committee, and they may submit reports, documentation or other information, both in writing and orally. Their cooperation has proved to be essential during the pre-sessional working group of the Committee. For that reason, the Committee decided that non-governmental organizations would be invited to the meetings of the working group with a view to providing it with expert advice. The Committee will address its invitations in the light of objective criteria, *i.e.* primarily based on written information previously submitted by non-governmental organizations (. . .). Such organisations will be expected to provide factual information on specific aspects of each State Party report under consideration, in the light of the guidelines for reporting adopted by the Committee, including on the level of their involvement in the process of the preparation of the report, as well as on the implementation of the Convention'.

On the role of NGOs in the reporting process and its benefits: see R. Brett, 'State Reporting: an NGO Perspective', in: A.F. Bayefsky (ed.), *The UN Human Rights System in the 21st Century* (The Hague/London/Boston, Kluwer Law International, 2000), pp. 57–62; A. Clapham, 'UN Human Rights Reporting Procedures: An NGO Perspective', in: Ph. Alston and J. Crawford (eds.), *The Future of Human Rights Treaty Monitoring* (Cambridge, Cambridge University Press, 2000), pp. 175–198; G. Lansdown, 'The reporting process under the Convention on the Rights of the Child', in: Ph. Alston and J. Crawford (eds.), *The Future of Human Rights Treaty Monitoring* (Cambridge, Cambridge University Press, 2000), pp. 118–122; and L. Theytaz-Bergman, 'State Reporting and the Role of Non-Governmental Organizations', in: A.F. Bayefsky (ed.), *The UN Human Rights System in the 21st Century* (The Hague/London/Boston, Kluwer Law International, 2000), pp. 45–56. See also *infra* No 41–43.

as well as the participation of NGOs and individual experts in its pre-sessional working group meetings.[110] These guidelines require that written contributions made by NGOs (or national coalitions or committees of NGOs) and individual experts and requests of NGOs to participate in the pre-sessional working group are to be submitted to the Committee through its Secretariat at least two months before the pre-session starts.[111] When doing so, the Committee members have the time to examine the remarks delivered by the NGOs and to compare these to the reports drawn up by the States. Based on the written information submitted, the Committee will issue a written invitation to selected NGOs[112] to participate in the pre-sessional working group.[113] The pre-session further also offers an opportunity for the children themselves to participate in the reporting procedure. The UNICEF programme 'What Do You Think?' made it possible for children to have their voices heard by the Committee. This was for instance the case for Belgian children, who drew up their own shadow report, on the basis of which they were invited by the Committee to take the floor during the pre-sessional working group.[114]

30. However, this way of working (the study of the reports by the Committee in several steps) did not turn out to be efficient in all cases. This is due to

---

[110] UN Doc. CRC/C/90, 1999, para. 320. For the text of these guidelines: see CRC Committee, *Guidelines for the participation of partners (NGOs and individual experts) in the pre-sessional working group of the Committee on the Rights of the Child* (UN Doc. CRC/C/90, 1999), Annex VIII. Also the NGO Group for the CRC drew up specific guidelines for NGO reporting: see http://www.crin.org/NGOGroupforCRC/.

[111] See CRC Committee, *Guidelines for the participation of partners (NGOs and individual experts) in the pre-sessional working group of the Committee on the Rights of the Child* (UN Doc. CRC/C/90, 1999), Annex VIII, paras. 2 and 3. Moreover, NGOs and individual experts wishing to provide written information to the Committee, should do so by providing twenty copies of each document to the Committee Secretariat (*Ibid.*, para. 2).

[112] The Committee will only invite NGOs whose information is particularly relevant to its consideration of the States Parties' reports. Priority will be given to partners who have provided information within the requested time-limit, who are working in the State Party concerned and who can provide first-hand information that is complementary to information already available to the Committee: see CRC Committee, *Guidelines for the participation of partners (NGOs and individual experts) in the pre-sessional working group of the Committee on the Rights of the Child* (UN Doc. CRC/C/90, 1999), Annex VIII, para. 4.

[113] CRC Committee, *Guidelines for the participation of partners (NGOs and individual experts) in the pre-sessional working group of the Committee on the Rights of the Child* (UN Doc. CRC/C/90, 1999), Annex VIII, para. 4. The Committee strongly recommends that its partners limit their introductory remarks, which should be limited to highlights of the written submission, to a maximum of 15 minutes for in – country NGOs and 5 minutes for others (*Ibid.*, para. 5).

[114] X., *That's my opinion . . . What Do You Think? First report by children and young people living in Belgium for the Committee on the Rights of the Child in Geneva*, UNICEF Belgium, 2001, 87 p. See on this: Y. Willemot, 'What do you think? Children Reporting on Children's Rights,' in: E. Verhellen and A. Weyts (eds.), *Understanding Children's Rights - 2003* (Children's Rights Centre, Ghent University, Ghent, 2004), pp. 271–286.

the fact that the pre-sessional working group often had to spend too much time gathering additional information.[115] Some of the States did not have sufficient time to prepare the additional information. In many cases, the information has been submitted on the day of the discussion, which made it necessary for the representatives to present the information orally.

Another concern, raised by NGOs, is the absence of a lot of Committee members at this pre-session, and the fact that the present ones are often unprepared.[116] Furthermore, the NGOs complain about the fact that there is no room for a real discussion during the pre-session.[117]

1.2.2   The Constructive Dialogue

31. In a second stage, the reports are discussed in an open, public, plenary meeting between the Committee members and the representatives of the reporting States. Anyone interested in the report can attend the meeting (NGO's, journalists, and other interested individuals) but only representatives of the UN bodies and agencies may ask the floor.

32. The Committee examines the reports, submitted by the various countries, on the basis of the pre-sessional working groups' preparations and the contributions made by the NGOs. The discussion begins with the presentation by the delegation of the reporting State on the answers to the list of issues, received from the pre-sessional working group. These presentations then lead to a dialogue in which the Committee members raise questions, make comments, ask for additional information and the delegates respond. It is not only the Committee's intention to check what rights the States have not implemented, but also to check whether those that have been implemented so far have been done so successfully.[118]

33. It is, however, not easy to have a profound and constructive dialogue on the basis of the – in most cases – lengthy and complex reports. The quality of the dialogue will always depend on several elements: the quality of the report, the document knowledge of the Committee members, the relevance of the questions asked, the available time, the priorities set, etc. The capacity of the representatives of the States is an important condition for a constructive dialogue. Hence, the Committee has more than once stressed

---

[115] A. Abramson, 'First State reports: Sunny and . . . cloudy', l.c. (note 95), p. 26.
[116] L. Theytaz-Bergman, 'State Reporting and the Role of Non-Governmental Organizations', l.c. (note 109), p. 54; G. Lansdown, l.c. (note 109), p. 124.
[117] G. Lansdown, l.c. (note 109), p. 124.
[118] D. Goodman, l.c. (note 94), p. 48.

that the States should delegate expert representatives in order to hold as efficient a dialogue as possible.[119]

34. The main problem the Committee is facing in order to have a good dialogue is an enormous lack of time due to the large number of ratifications of the CRC. The current way of proceeding impedes the Committee to hold a fair dialogue with the States' delegates, and yields to failure of the Committee to consider the reports within a reasonable time.[120] In order to resolve these problems to a certain extent, the Committee has taken some measures.[121] Firstly, the Committee gradually increased the number of reports it has to review during each session. The original six reports per session became eight,[122] nine or ten per session. Secondly, the Committee gradually reduced the amount of hours it can at the most spend on the discussion of one report. Since its 25th session, a maximum of 6 hours – instead of nine hours –[123] are spent on one report. Thirdly, the Committee decided that the States Parties should, in the drafting of the reports, focus on the most important issues, as indicated by the Committee in its last concluding observations.[124] Also the 'list of issues', drawn up by the pre-sessional working group, should be

---

[119] UN Doc. CRC/C/10, 1992, para. 40; L. Theytaz-Bergman, 'Adjustments urgently needed. Fourth session of the Committee on the Rights of the Child', l.c. (note 95), p. 22; Clapham points at the fact that NGOs could play an important role in getting the right persons representing the government: A. Clapham, l.c. (note 109), p. 189.

[120] The Committee decided during its first meeting that each report should be responded to within one year after submission: see T. Hammarberg, 'Justice for Children through the UN-Convention', in : S. Asquith and M. Hill (eds.), Justice for Children (Dordrecht/Boston/London, Martinus Nijhoff Publishers, 1994), p. 69. However, often there is a backlog of one to sometimes more than two years of reports waiting to be reviewed: see G. Lansdown, l.c. (note 109), p. 125.

[121] Some of these measures were already withdrawn as they appeared to be inefficient. For instance, the request of the Committee to the States to submit written answers to the questions of the pre-sessional working group and to send them to the Committee beforehand was withdrawn as most of the States did not have sufficient time (only 1 month) to prepare the additional information and consequently only submitted their answers at the day of the session itself and sometimes only in their own language: see L. Theytaz-Bergman, 'Out of time. 5th session of the Committee on the Rights of the Child', International children's rights monitor 11, No 1, 1994, p. 10.

[122] During the 23rd session, the Committee considered for the first time eight – instead of the six – reports per session, see UN Doc. CRC/C/87, 1999, para. 255.

[123] It was in the course of the fifth session (1994) that the Committee decided to spend at the most 9 hours on the discussion of each single country report: see L. Theytaz-Bergman, 'Out of time. 5th session of the Committee on the Rights of the Child', l.c. (note 121), p. 11.

[124] UN Doc. CRC/C/69, 1997. see also CRC Committee, Recommendation on the Organization of Work (UN Doc. CRC/C/118, 2002), pp. 4–5.

limited to the main issues.[125] In this way, the most flagrant problems regarding the situation of children in that particular country can certainly be dealt with. Finally, the Committee decided to re-establish the system of 'country-rapporteurs'.[126] The Committee thus clearly makes efforts to spend its available time as efficiently as possible. However, in doing this, it is confronted with a dilemma: on the one hand, it is forced to limit its backlog to a minimum; on the other hand, it should get a sufficient overview of the children's rights' situation in the country in order to be able to make recommendations. In approaching this dilemma, the Committee may not forget its own basic principle: the first objective pursued through the reporting is to promote respect for human rights and ensure genuine accountability by means of a constructive dialogue with the States, which is time-consuming.[127] However, until now, the Committee opted for the time limit, at the cost of the quality of the dialogues. In some cases, and in the opinion of Theytaz-Bergman, the time limit has had some baleful influences on the Committee's activities: 'This (the time limit) proved to be disastrous in the case of Mexico where the Committee barely had time to even touch upon the serious problems that the country is facing including street children, torture and the uprising in the Chiapas region'.[128] A measure that might succeed in following both paths is the recent extension of the Committee members from 10 to 18 and its foreseen split into two chambers, for a period of two years, from 2005 onwards.[129]

While it is up to the Committee to get its priorities right by constant review of its working methods, some more radical changes will be needed in the long run in order to really eliminate the backlog.[130]

---

[125] Announced by Mrs Tigerstedt-Tähtelä, former member of the CRC Committee, during her talk on 13 December 2000, at the fifth 'International Interdisciplinary Course on Children's Rights', organised in Ghent by the Children's Rights Centre of the Ghent University. This issue was touched upon during the 22nd session (UN Doc. CRC/C/90, 1999), para. 319.

[126] UN Docs. CRC/C/90, 1999, para. 318 and CRC/C/87, 1999, para. 255. The country rapporteur is responsible: (1) for the contact with the staff member of the secretariat throughout the whole process; (2) for leading the discussion during the pre-session and the session; (3) for finalising the list of issues to be addressed to the State Party after the pre-sessional working group meeting and (4) for finalising and ensuring the quality of the concluding observations and recommendations.

[127] Ph. Alston, *Effective functioning of Bodies established pursuant to United Nations human rights instruments. Final report on enhancing the long-term effectiveness of the United Nations human rights treaty system* (UN doc. E/CN/4/1997/74, 1997), Annex, para. 52.

[128] J. Smith, 'The Committee on the Rights of the Child', *Netherlans Quarterly of Human Rights*, 1994, p. 322; L. Theytaz-Bergman, 'Out of time. 5th session of the Committee on the Rights of the Child', *l.c.* (note 121), p. 11.

[129] *Cf. supra* No 9.

[130] *Cf. infra* No 55.

1.2.3 *The Concluding Observations*

35. In a final stage of the reporting procedure, the Committee prepares its concluding observations on the report in a private meeting.[131] As pointed out in Article 45(d) of the CRC, the Committee is indeed allowed to 'make suggestions and general recommendations, based on information received pursuant to Articles 44 and 45'. The concluding observations contain a general evaluation of the report and the main points of the dialogue with the delegation. They underline the positive developments that have been noted to have taken place during the period under review. At the same time they indicate the topics that require a special follow-up; which makes the concluding observation the basis for the discussion of the reports that follow. The observations are sent to the State Party concerned and reported to the General Assembly.[132]

36. The concluding observations concerning the initial reports are always structured in one and the same way:[133] (1) introduction; (2) positive aspects; (3) factors and difficulties impeding the implementation of the Convention; (4) principal subjects of concern; (5) suggestions and recommendations.[134] Since the nineteenth session however, the distinction until then made between (4) principal subjects of concern and (5) suggestions and recommendations has disappeared and has been replaced by the single (4) (principal) subject(s) of concern and the Committee's recommendations.

The structure of the concluding observations of the periodic reports is the following:[135] (1) introduction; (2) follow-up measures undertaken and progress achieved by the State Party; (3) factors and difficulties impeding

---

[131] UN Doc. CRC/C/10, 1992, para. 41. For an entire overview of the 'concluding observations' from the 1th until the 17th session: L. Holmström (ed.), *Concluding Observations of the UN Committee on the Rights of the Child* (The Hague, Martinus Nijhoff Publishers, 1999), 600 p.; See also the 'UN Treaty Bodies Database' for the concluding observations: http://www.ohchr.org/.

[132] The information will possibly be accompanied by comments, if any, from the States Parties (Article 45(d) of the CRC).

[133] *E. g.* UN Docs. CRC/C/80, 1998; CRC/C/84, 1999; CRC/C/87, 1999; CRC/C/90, 1999. However, there are some exceptions to the rule: *E.g.* CRC Committee, *Concluding Observations: Austria* (UN Doc. CRC/C/84, 1999), paras 29–59; and *the Netherlands* (UN Doc. CRC/C/90, 1999), paras. 232–262. The concluding observations to the reports of these States consist of three parts only (instead of four): (1) introduction; (2) positive aspects and (3) principal subjects of concern and the Committee's recommendations. The fourth part 'factors and difficulties impeding the implementation of the Convention' has been omitted.

[134] UN Doc. CRC/C/10, 1992, para. 42.

[135] There are some exceptions to the rule: During the twentieth session, for instance, when considering the periodic report of Sweden, and during the twenty-second session, when considering the periodic report of the Russian Federation the fourth element 'factors and difficulties impeding further progress in the implementation of the Convention' has been

further progress in the implementation of the Convention; and (4) principal subjects of concern and the Committee's recommendations.

37. The exact formulation of the concluding observations is an important condition for the success of the reporting procedure.[136] They must not be drawn up too cautiously as this may lead to indifference of States regarding the follow-up of the recommendations. But the Committee must also be careful that is observations do not turn into convictions because it does not have the authority to do so.[137] It is not only the formulation of the concluding observations but also the follow-up of suggestions and recommendations that is of paramount importance.[138] Therefore, the Committee encourages the States to publish the concluding observations made on their report.[139]

38. The legal effects of concluding observations are rather weak. Concluding observations are not binding on the States Parties. They contain mere suggestions and recommendations to come closer to the implementation of the CRC, but no binding judgments. As Dimitrijevic rightly points out, concluding observations do not amount to condemnation for non-fulfilment of treaty obligations, even if they contain strong statements indicating that the Convention has not been complied with by the State.[140] However, like general comments, they contain the view of the CRC Committee – which can be considered as the most authoritative body monitoring the Convention – as a whole. Therefore, concluding observations cannot easily be ignored and should serve as a basis for action of the States Parties, UN bodies, and other competent organs, such as NGOs.[141]

---

omitted. See CRC Committee, *Concluding Observations: Sweden* (UN Doc. CRC/C/84, 1999), paras. 128–150; and *the Russian Federation* (UN Doc. CRC/C/90, 1999), paras. 63–135.

[136] See also one of the principal recommendations in the study carried out by Philip Alston by order of the General Assembly of the UN: Ph. Alston, *Effective functioning of Bodies established pursuant to United Nations human rights instruments. Final report on enhancing the long-term effectiveness of the United Nations human rights treaty system, o.c.* (note 127), para. 122: 'Treaty bodies must strive to further improve the quality of their 'concluding observations', in terms of clarity, degree of detail, level of accuracy and specificity'.

[137] For a case that can be discussed and in which the Committee nearly surpassed its authorities, see concerning the report of Sudan: A. Abramson, 'First State reports: Sunny and . . . cloudy', *l.c.* (note 95), p. 24.

[138] The Committee has emphasised that a follow-up of the suggestions and recommendations is really necessary See UN Doc. CRC/C/20, 1993, para. 28. See also CRC Committee, *Follow up to the consideration of initial reports by States Parties to the convention of the Rights of the Child as at 24 February 1994* (UN Doc. CRC/C/27, 1994), Annex.

[139] UN Doc. CRC/C/20, 1993, para. 29.

[140] V. Dimitrijevic, *l.c.* (note 77), p. 198.

[141] On the moral authority of concluding observations: See I. Boerefijn, 'The Human Rights Committee's Concluding Observations', in: M. Castermans – Holleman, F. Van Hoof and J. Smith (eds.), *The role of the nation-state in the 21st century, foreign policy, human rights, international*

1.3   A Cooperative Approach to Implementation

1.3.1   Technical Assistance and Advice

39. As has been pointed out above, the drafters of the CRC did not want a purely controlling monitoring mechanism. The reporting procedure should at the same time be a tool in order to act in an advisory or assisting way wherever needed. This is reflected in Article 45(b) of the CRC, which adds a peculiar procedure to the reporting mechanism.[142]

The Committee can send reports that contain a request or show a need for technical support to specialised agencies, UNICEF and other competent bodies. The Committee itself decides whether the reports will be transmitted or not. In this regard, the CRC goes a step further than other treaties, like *e.g.* the CCPR[143] and the CESCR,[144] where the Committees have to make a request to the Secretary-General who then takes the initiative. In most cases, the CRC Committee refers to bodies and agencies inside the UN; in only a few cases it refers to intergovernmental organisations and international or regional NGOs.[145]

When a need for technical support appears to be necessary, the Committee will encourage the State Party to discuss the proposed programme with the supporting agency.[146] In its Rules of Procedure, the Committee also expressed the intention to do a follow-up of the reports that have been transmitted: it may request the information on the technical advice or assistance – provided and the progress achieved.[147] Technical assistance may consist of *inter alia* assistance in law reform, training of personnel on how to draw up a report, development and establishment of programmes on how to implement the CRC, expert services to create internal infrastructure and the organisation of conferences.

40. No other human rights instrument links reporting with development cooperation to such a large extent.[148] Moreover, the Committee encourages

---

organisations (The Hague, Kluwer, 1998), pp. 232 and 248; and I. Boerefijn, *The Reporting Procedure under the Covenant on Civil and Political Rights: Practice and Procedures of the Human Rights Committee* (Antwerpen-Groningen-Oxford, Intersentia-Hart, 1999), pp. 303–304.

[142] See also CRC Committee, *the Provisional Rules of Procedure* (UN Doc. CRC/C/4, 1991), Rule 74.

[143] Article 40(3) of the CCPR.

[144] Article16(2)(b) of the CESCR.

[145] *E.g.* UN Doc. CRC/C/40/Rev. 16, 2000.

[146] UN Doc. CRC/C/16, 1993, par. 144. See also CRC Committee, *the Provisional Rules of Procedure* (UN Doc. CRC/C/4, 1991), Rule 74.

[147] D. Goodman, *l.c.* (note 94), p. 53. See also UN Doc. CRC/C/40/Rev.4, 1996.

[148] T. Hammarberg, *l.c.* (note 120), p. 70.

the States Parties, through its concluding observations, to look for, or to render, international assistance.[149] In this way, also the reporting procedure can develop into an important basis for well-founded development policies. Also Article 4 of the CRC embodies the idea of mutual help and support: '(. . .) With regard to economic, social and cultural rights, States Parties shall undertake such measures to the maximum extent of their available resources and, where needed, within the framework of international cooperation'. Other articles containing a strong plea for international cooperation in order to implement the CRC's provisions are 23(4) and 24(4) and 28(3) of the CRC.

1.3.2 *Partnership with Other Bodies*

41. The cooperative spirit of the Convention also lies in the fact that the Committee involves other agencies and organisations from inside and outside the UN in the reporting procedure. Article 45(a) of the CRC deals with the relationship between the Committee and these bodies and places this relationship in two categories: *mandated* and *on Committee invitation*.[150] UN bodies and agencies are *entitled* to be represented when the Committee is considering the implementation of any of the Convention's provisions that 'fall within the mandate' of that body. It is only on the Committee's *invitation*, however, that other bodies can share in its monitoring task. These other bodies are then invited to give their expert advise. The term 'other competent bodies' should be understood in the broadest sense, including NGOs, organisations on a regional level (such as the Council of Europe, the African Union, the Organisation of American States), national research institutions etc.[151] The Committee can of course also *invite* the specialised agencies and UNICEF to give expert advise in areas falling within the scope of their mandate. Furthermore, it can ask all the above mentioned bodies to submit reports. The CRC thus constitutes a broad basis for participation for

---

[149] *E.g.* CRC Committee, *Concluding Observations: Sudan* (UN Doc. CRC/C/20, 1993), para. 119; *Peru* (UN Doc. CRC/C/20, 1993), para. 73; *Jordan* (UN Doc. CRC/C/97, 2000), para. 200; *Côte d'Ivoire* (UN Doc. CRC/C/108, 2001), para. 338; *Kenya* (UN Doc. CRC/C/111, 2001), para. 135; *Cameroon* (UN Doc. CRC/C/111, 2001), para. 380; *Gambia* (UN Doc. CRC/C/111, 2001), para. 453; *Guinea-Bissau* (UN Doc. CRC/C/118, 2002), para. 75.

[150] A.G. Mower, Jr., *The Convention on the Rights of the Child, International Law Support for Children* (London, Greenwood Press, 1997), pp. 66–67. See also CRC Committee, *the Provisional Rules of Procedure* (UN Doc. CRC/C/4, 1991), Rule 34.

[151] See the *Travaux Préparatoires*: S. Detrick (ed.), *The United Nations Convention on the Rights of the Child: A Guide to the "Travaux Préparatoires"*, *o.c.* (note 20), p. 582; see also CRC Committee, *Guidelines for the participation of partners (NGOs and individual experts) in the pre-sessional working group of the Committee on the Rights of the Child* (UN Doc. CRC/C/90, 1999), Annex VIII, para. 1.

all kinds of organisations in the monitoring process. In view of the increase in the number of treaties on human rights, of control bodies and control procedures, both within the UN and on a regional level, the explicit inclusion of this matter is an important and innovative aspect of the reporting procedure and an important opportunity to come to a certain degree of coordination and cooperation.

42. In view of the workload, the limited financial resources of the Committee Secretariat,[152] and the fact that governments are inherently limited when attempting to indicate 'factors and difficulties' in the country they represent, the Committee needs to use this possibility in order to become well-informed, and to attain a 'comprehensive understanding of the children's rights situation in a certain country.[153] These organisations indeed can provide the Committee with relevant information and documentation, assist it with identifying key issues in country reports, give information about the type and appropriateness of technical assistance, submit alternative reports, provide the Committee with reports and studies on topics or themes that are of particular interest to the Committee and assist in formulating the general comments.[154] Based on this input, the Committee can check whether the information obtained from the governments complies with the realities on the ground.

The Committee has responded to this unique provision by encouraging other bodies to participate in the reporting procedure. It periodically exchanges views with other UN bodies and agencies[155] and is quite progressive in its cooperation with NGOs.[156] The cooperation with the latter was enhanced by adopting guidelines on the basis of which NGOs can address the Committee on issues regarding specific country reports during the pre-sessional working group.[157] The CRC Committee has the advantage of being supported by the NGO Group for the CRC which aims to facilitates the flow

---

[152] UN Doc. CRC/C/10, 1992, paras. 27–28.

[153] See V. Dimitrijevic, l.c. (note 77), p. 192.

[154] D. Goodman, l.c. (note 94), pp. 57–58.

[155] See Ph. Alston, *Effective functioning of the bodies established pursuant to United Nations Human Rights Instruments. Final report on enhancing the long-term effectiveness of the United Nations human rights treaty system, o.c.* (note 127), para. 107: 'There are several outstanding examples of such co-operation, most notably between the Committee on the Rights of the Child and UNICEF, ILO, UNESCO and UNHCR (...)'.

[156] The Committee holds meetings with the coordinator of the of the NGO Ad Hoc Group (*E.g.* UN Doc. CRC/C/20, 1993, para. 172). *Cf. supra* No 29.

[157] *Cf. supra* No 29.

of information between the NGO community and the Committee.[158] The
Committee also seeks to cooperate with the other treaty bodies,[159] special
rapporteurs/representatives, experts and chairpersons of working groups
of the Human Rights Commission.[160] The Committee hence definitely made
efforts and created important advances. Some authors nevertheless point
at the fact that the Committee should play a more active role by reaching
out to the UN agencies, conferences and field operations rather than expect-
ing the agencies to come to its meetings.[161]

43. It should be stressed that the partnership is mutual. NGOs in their turn
use the reporting procedure to raise awareness about the rights of the child
and to promote realisation of these rights.[162] Also, the encouragement of
participation of the UN bodies and agencies to the reporting process made
the CRC a focal point in the activities and programmes of these bodies.[163]

2   Other Activities of the CRC Committee

2.1   Urgent Actions

44. One of the weaknesses of the reporting procedure is the fact that the
Committee is only authorised to act when it has a report at its disposal.
This means that in situations of grave human rights violations, the Committee

---

[158] L. Theytaz-Bergman, 'State Reporting and the Role of Non-Governmental Organizations',
l.c. (note 109), pp. 47–48 and 52.
[159] In order to come to some kind of cooperation, an annual meeting is held between the
Chairpersons of the Human Rights Treaty Bodies. Issues addressed at these meetings have
included, among other things, the streamlining and overall improvement of human rights
reporting procedures, harmonization of the Committee's methods of work, follow-up to
World Conferences, and financial issues. Since 2002, an Inter-Committee Meeting, consisting of the chairpersons plus two members of each of the committees, has also been convened to discuss these issues. Harmonization of working methods among Committees was
the main focus of the first Inter-Committee Meeting. The increased level of participation of
each of the Committees allowed for more detailed discussion of recommendations on issues
relating to working methods than had been possible in the Annual Chairpersons Meeting
because of time constraints. See http://www.ohchr.org.
[160] E.g. CRC Committee, Conclusions and Recommendations adopted on Relations with other United
Nations bodies and treaty bodies (UN Doc. CRC/C/10, 1992), pp. 4–5; CRC Committee, Conclusions
and Recommendations adopted on Relations with other United Nations bodies and treaty bodies (UN
Doc. CRC/C/16, 1993), pp. 5–6; CRC Committee, Conclusions and Recommendations adopted on
Relations with other United Nations bodies and treaty bodies (UN Doc. CRC/C/20, 1993), p. 6.
[161] A. Clapham, l.c. (note 109), p. 195.
[162] The encouragement of NGO participation to the reporting procedure yielded to a/o
more promotion at the domestic level through e.g. the publicity surround the alternative
NGO report and to the creation of national NGO coalitions: See G. Lansdown, l.c. (note 109),
pp. 120–122.
[163] J. Karp, l.c. (note 83), p. 42.

is in principle not able to undertake action and has to wait until the time has come for the submission of the report by the country concerned. In 1992, the members of the Committee therefore agreed upon the fact that the Committee, apart from the periodical study of the country reports, should also be authorised to undertake urgent actions in serious situations.[164] In practice, this means that the Committee can send letters to the government concerned, ask information, ask to draw up a report relating to the infringed right and create awareness of the particular topic by using the media and other channels. The Committee may also suggest a visit to the country concerned.[165]

45. Urgent actions should, however, continue to embody the spirit of the constructive dialogue. So, also when taking an urgent action, the Committee tries to take a non-conflicting stance. Moreover, a number of conditions have to be met, before the Committee is allowed to take urgent actions:[166]

(1) The action is to be based on reliable information. This information can be passed on by anybody (*e.g.* NGOs), provided that it is accurate and trustworthy;
(2) A violation of the rights undertaken in the CRC is to be involved. The problematic situation should fall within the jurisdiction of one of the States Parties;
(3) The violation concerned must be blatant. There must be a real danger that more violations will take place. It must be possible to avoid a deterioration of the situation by taking the urgent action.

46. As the Committee can ask a State at any time to draw up a report relating to the implementation of a specific provision of the Convention or to provide additional information, the urgent actions procedure is considered to be a part of the obligation to report.[167] However, the procedure could also be seen as alternative for the individual communications procedure. Indeed, the Committee has stressed that, apart from the UN organs, also other competent bodies can pass on blatant violations of the children's rights to the Committee. Since NGOs are generally accepted as competent bodies, they have the possibility to lodge a complaint with the Committee. Moreover, the conditions to start the 'urgent actions' – procedure are very

---

[164] UN Doc. CRC/C/10, 1992, paras. 54–58; B. Abramson, 'Un immense défi. Deuxieme session du Comité des Droits de l'Enfant', *Tribune internationale des droits de l'enfant* 9, No. 3–4, 1992, p. 24.
    A similar decision was taken by the Human Rights Committee: see UN Doc. CCPR/C/3/Rev.7, 2004, Rule 66(2); and the CERD Committee: see UN Doc. A/48/18, 1993, Annex III.
[165] UN Doc. CRC/C/10, 1992, para. 56.
[166] UN Doc. CRC/C/10, 1992, paras. 54–55.
[167] UN Doc. CRC/C/10, 1992, para. 56.

similar to the admissibility requirements of 'jurisdictional procedures': the violation must be blatant, it must be possible to avoid a deterioration of the situation and the action is to be based on reliable information. But then again, it remains unclear in which cases the Committee will declare a request for urgent actions admissible.

47. Although the increasing number of requests, urgent actions were taken in only a few occasions.[168] However, the Committee sometimes responded to serious violations of human rights by passing them on to other competent organs.[169] This has happened for example with a request for urgent actions (November 16, 1993) made by the Government of the Federal Republic of Yugoslavia. The Government asked the Committee to examine the violations of children's rights in Yugoslavia as a consequence of the sanctions imposed by the UN. The Committee passed the case on to the Special Rapporteur on the former Yugoslavia, since it did not have sufficient information on this matter at its disposal.[170]

2.2   Studies on Topics concerning the Rights of the Child

48. The Committee can initiate research on specific themes regarding the rights of the child.

In the first place, it can make a request for studies to organs inside and outside the UN. Article 45(c) of the CRC states that the Committee may recommend to the General Assembly of the UN to request the Secretary-General to undertake on its behalf studies on specific issues relating to the rights

---

[168] *E.g.* In November 1991, the Committee sent an urgent recommendation to the Government of Indonesia requesting information on the excessive use of violence by security forces against demonstrating children in Santa Cruz, Dili: see UN Doc. CRC/C/20, 1993, para. 52.

[169] UN Doc. CRC/C/10, 1992, para. 57. Also Alston is in favour of this cautious way of handling: See Ph. Alston, *Effective functioning of Bodies established pursuant to United Nations human rights instruments. Final report on enhancing the long-term effectiveness of the United Nations human rights treaty system, o.c.* (note 127), paras. 79 and 119: '(. . .) there is much to be said for maintaining what has been referred to as 'a division of labour . . . whereby the special rapporteurs, representatives or experts [of the Commission of Human Rights, etc.] would remain responsible for urgent appeals, whereas the treaty bodies would focus mainly on State Party reports' (para. 79) – 'In general, the division of labour between the treaty bodies and special mechanisms should be maintained' (para. 119).

[170] X, 'Federal Republic of Yugoslavia. Urgent Action requested', *International children's rights monitor* 10, No 4, 1993, p. 25. For a critical view on this case, see M. O'Flaherty, 'Treaty bodies responding to states of emergency: The case of Bosnia and Herzegovina', in: Ph. Alston and J. Crawford, *The Future of UN Human Rights Treaty Monitoring* (Cambridge, Cambridge University Press, 2000), pp. 458–459.

of the child.[171] When reading this provision together with Article 45(a) of the CRC, it becomes clear that the Committee can make the same request to specialised agencies, UNICEF, and other bodies.[172] The advantage of such studies is that they can be used to establish the facts in matters of urgency without having to wait the full reporting cycle. Furthermore, they contribute to an increased awareness and better understanding of the provisions of the Convention and their implementation.[173]

In the second place, the Committee regularly dedicates a day to the study of a specific topic: it holds a day of general discussion.[174] The chosen topics usually reflect the Committee's major concerns regarding the States Parties' reports.[175] As of November 2004, the following themes have been discussed: children in armed conflicts,[176] economic exploitation of children,[177] the role of the family in the promotion of the rights of the child,[178] the girl child,[179] the administration of juvenile justice,[180] the child and the media,[181]

---

[171] See also CRC Committee, *the Provisional Rules of Procedure* (UN Doc. CRC/C/4, 1991), Rule 76.

E.g. the Committee has recommended to the General Assembly of the UN to request the Secretary-General to carry out a study on 'children in armed conflicts': CRC Committee, *Children in armed conflicts: Recommendation to the General Assembly*: see UN Docs. CRC/C/16, 1993, p. 4; and A/51/306. Another request has been done for a study on violence against children, which is currently under preparation. In September 2004, the Committee asked the Commission on Human Rights to consider establishing a working group to prepare draft United Nations guidelines for the protection and alternative care of children without parental care, for adoption by 2008. To this end, the Committee requested the Office of the United Nations High Commissioner for Human Rights, the United Nations Children's Fund, the World Health Organization, other interested intergovernmental bodies and international non-governmental organizations to provide information and support to the working group. See UN Doc. CRC/C/143, 2005, pp. 4–5.

[172] D. Goodman, *l.c.* (note 94), p. 54.

[173] UN Doc. CRC/C/10, 1992, para. 59. See also UN Doc. CRC/C/16, 1993, para. 147.

[174] CRC Committee, *the Provisional Rules of Procedure* (UN Doc. CRC/C/4, 1991), Rule 75.

[175] J. Karp, *l.c.* (note 83), p. 39.

[176] CRC Committee, *Day of General Discussion on children in armed conflict* (UN Docs. CRC/C/10, 1992, paras. 61–77; and CRC/C/16, 1993, paras. 173–180). See also: B. Abramson, 'Un immense défi. Deuxieme session du Comité des Droits de l'Enfant', *l.c.* (note 164), p. 24.

[177] CRC Committee, *Day of General Discussion on the economic exploitation of children* (UN Docs. CRC/C/20, 1993, paras. 186–196; and CRC/C/24, 1994, paras. 176–177).

[178] CRC Committee, *Day of General Discussion on the role of the family in the promotion of the rights of the child* (UN Doc. CRC/C/34, 1994), paras. 183–201.

[179] CRC Committee, *Day of General Discussion on the Girl Child* (UN Docs. CRC/C/38, 1995), paras. 275–299.

[180] CRC Committee, *Day of General Discussion on the administration of juvenile justice* (UN Doc. CRC/C/46, 1995), paras. 203–238.

[181] CRC Committee, *Day of General Discussion on the child and the media* (UN Doc. CRC/C/57, 1996), paras. 242–257.

the rights of the child with disabilities,[182] children living in a world with HIV/AIDS,[183] State violence against children, violence against children within the family and at school,[184] the private sector as service provider and its role in implementing child rights,[185] the rights of indigenous children,[186] and implementing child rights in early childhood.[187] The debate is held within the spirit of partnership with UN agencies and bodies, NGOs, individual experts and other competent bodies. Sometimes also government's representatives are present.[188] On the basis of the debate, the Committee formulates its recommendations. The thematic days yield to a uniform interpretation of the provisions of the Convention, led to the adoption of additional protocols to the Convention,[189] and constitute a basis for the issuing of general comments on specific provisions of the Convention.

2.3   General Comments

49. Unlike the CCPR,[190] the CRC does not explicitly refer to the formulation of 'general comments' as one of the Committee's responsibilities.[191] As from its establishment, the Committee nevertheless considered this as one of its tasks.[192] However, it took ten years before the first general comment was adopted.[193] This happened during the Committee's 26th session in January 2001. It was Article 29 of the Convention, containing the aims of education,

---

[182] CRC Committee, *Day of General Discussion on Children with Disabilities* (UN Docs. CRC/C/66, 1997, Annex V, paras. 328–329; CRC/C/69, 1997, paras. 310–339; CRC/C/73, 1998, paras. 171–172; CRC/C/80, 1998, paras. 244–247; and CRC/C/87, 1999, paras. 272–275).

[183] CRC Committee, *Day of General Discussion on Children living in a World with AIDS* (UN Doc. CRC/C/80, 1998), paras. 210–243.

[184] CRC Committee, *Day of General Discussion on violence against children in the family and at school* (UN Doc. CRC/C/111, 2001), paras. 674–745 and Annex VIII.

[185] CRC Committee, *Day of General Discussion on the private sector as service provider and its role in implementing child rights* (UN Doc. CRC/C/121, 2002), paras. 630–653 and Annex II.

[186] CRC Committee, *Day of General Discussion on the Rights of Indigenous Children* (UN Doc. CRC/C/133, 2003), paras. 608–624.

[187] CRC Committee, *Day of General Discussion on Implementing child rights in early childhood*, (UN Doc. CRC/C/137, 2004), paras. 8–9, and (UN Doc. CRC/C/143, 2005), paras. 532–563.

[188] J. Karp, *l.c.* (note 83), p. 39.

[189] *E.g.*, the Day of General Discussion on children in armed conflict has led to the adoption of an optional protocol. See UN Doc. CRC/C/16, 1993, Annex VII.

[190] Article 40(4) of the CCPR.

[191] Article 45 of the CRC only states that the Committee may make 'suggestions and general recommendations' – which is reiterated in Rules 71 and 72 of the Provisional Rules of Procedure (UN Doc. CRC/C/4, 1991) – without mentioning 'general comments'.

[192] CRC Committee, *the Provisional Rules of Procedure* (UN Doc. CRC/C/4, 1991), Rule 73.

[193] During its sixth session (1994), the Committee decided to postpone the adoption of general comments. Being young at the time, the Committee faced its teething problems and deemed it necessary to assemble some further experience before the provisions and principles

that was chosen to be commented upon.[194] The fact that the article reflects the central spirit of the Convention[195] and contains values, relevant for the debates held at that time at the World Conference on Racism,[196] may explain the eventual choice of the Committee. As of November 2004, the Committee has adopted five general comments. The second one regards the role of independent national human rights institutions in the promotion and protection of the rights of the child,[197] the third one looks upon HIV/AIDS and the rights of the child,[198] General Comment No 4 deals with adolescent health and development[199] and General Comment No 5 regards the general measures of implementation for the CRC.[200] At the moment, the Committee is drafting four other general comments (juvenile justice, asylum – seeking and separated children, rights of indigenous children and rights of children with disabilities).

50. General comments are based upon the experience gained so far through the examination of reports. The Committee summarises its findings and makes them available for the benefit of all States Parties. Several types of

---

of the Convention could be interpreted in the form of general comments: see UN Doc. CRC/C/29, 1994, para. 184. Besides inexperience, another reason for the postponement is that the time factor does not play a crucial role, as is the case for the examination of the States' reports and the formulation of the concluding observations: see E. Tistounet, 'The problem of overlapping among different treaty bodies', in: Ph. Alston and J. Crawford, *The Future of UN Human Rights Treaty Monitoring* (Cambridge, Cambridge University Press, 2000), p. 395. During its seventeenth session (1998), the Committee raked up the issue and decided to begin preparing them: see UN Doc. CRC/C/73, 1998, para. 149. From then on several intentions were uttered. The subject it planned to comment on shifted from the rights of disabled children (Article 23 of the CRC) to the participation rights (Articles 12 to 17 of the CRC) and then again to the aims of education (Article 29(1) of the CRC). See UN Docs. CRC/C/84, 1999, para. 221, sub c; CRC/C/90, 1999, para. 291, sub w and CRC/C/94, 2000, para 480.

[194] UN Doc. CRC/C/103, 2001, para. 575; For the text of this general comment, see CRC Committee, *General Comment No 1 on the Aims of Education* (UN Doc. CRC/GC/2001/1, 2001).

[195] CRC Committee, *General Comment No 1 on the Aims of Education* (UN Doc. CRC/GC/2001/1, 2001), para. 1.

[196] The World Conference against Racism, Racial Discrimination, Xenophobia and Related Intolerance, held in Durban, South Africa, from 31 August to 7 September 2001. See UN Docs. CRC/C/94, 2000, para 480 and CRC/SP/31, 2000, para. 6(c)(iv).

[197] CRC Committee, *General Comment No 2 (2002) The role of independent national human rights institutions in the promotion and protection of the rights of the child* (UN Doc. CRC/GC/2002/2, 2002).

[198] CRC Committee, *General Comment No 3 (2003) HIV/AIDS and the rights of the Child* (UN Doc. CRC/GC/2003/3, 2003).

[199] CRC Committee, *General Comment No 4 (2003) Adolescent Health and development in the context of the Convention on the Rights of the Child* (UN Doc. CRC/GC/2003/4, 2003).

[200] CRC Committee, *General Comment No 5 (2003) General measures of implementation for the Convention on the Rights of the Child* (UN Doc. CRC/GC/2003/5, 2003).

general comments can be distinguished: (1) those, which give interpretations of specific articles, (2) those that deal with general issues, such as the reporting obligations, the issue of reservations, etc., and (3) those that are rather thematic. Unlike the CESCR Committee, the CRC Committee dedicated its first general comment to the interpretation of a specific article instead of explaining the reporting obligation. The second general comment of the CRC Committee could be considered as a partly interpretation of Article 4 of the CRC. The third and the fourth general comment are thematic as they deal with an overlapping theme that touches upon several articles of the Convention (*i.e.* HIV/AIDS and adolescent health respectively). The fifth general comment, explaining the general implementation measures, is of a general nature.

51. The purpose of general comments coincides with the Committee's *raison d'être*, being the improvement of the implementation of the CRC's provisions by guiding the governments on the implementation of its norms. To this end, general comments attempt to enhance the understanding of the rights enshrined in the Convention and draw attention to the insufficiencies disclosed by a large number of reports; they illuminate the States Parties' obligations, aim at stimulating the implementation activities of the governments and relevant international bodies as well as try to clarify the reporting requirements.

52. The impact of the general comments is difficult to determine. Still, some reflections on their potential implications are worth mentioning. General comments are not binding on the States. However, considering the impact of general comments formulated by other treaty bodies, it can be expected that the CRC's general comments will, similarly, have great moral authority.[201] General comments contain the view of the Committee – being the most authoritative body monitoring the Convention – as a whole and are addressed to all States Parties. They hence constitute an authoritative interpretation of the rights enshrined in the Convention. The interpretations made by the Committee, although technically not binding, should therefore be given

---

[201] The moral authority of general comments has been stressed by several authors. With regard to the Human Rights Committee: see I. Boerefijn, *The Reporting Procedure under the Covenant on Civil and Political Rights: Practice and Procedures of the Human Rights Committee, o.c.* (note 141), pp. 294 and 300; See also Y. Iwasawa, 'The domestic impact of international human rights standards: the Japanese experience', in: Ph. Alston and J. Crawford (eds.), *The Future of UN Human Rights Treaty Monitoring* (Cambridge, Cambridge University Press, 2000), pp. 258–259; and M. Nowak, *U.N. Covenant on Civil and Political Rights - CCPR Commentary, o.c.* (note 81), p. XXIV, para. 21 and p. 576.

considerable weight in the identification of the scope of the rights and obligations enshrined in the CRC. Further, the illuminating function of general comments could positively influence international monitoring. General comments could in the first place enhance the reporting behaviour of the governments to the CRC Committee.[202] But they could also be a source of inspiration for other monitoring bodies when monitoring equivalent provisions in the respective Conventions. Furthermore, the significance of general comments for the debate on the possible adoption of an individual complaints procedure under the CESCR must be underlined here. It has been argued that a better understanding and larger awareness of social, economic and cultural rights could lead to a more open attitude towards the justifiability of this generation of rights and could positively influence the debate on an individual petitioning system.[203] As also the CRC's social, economic and cultural rights are an obstacle for the incorporation of an individual complaints procedure into the Convention,[204] the advocates of an individual petition right under the CRC could copy this argument. General comments can finally serve as a frame of reference for the domestic courts when interpreting the education articles of the CRC.[205] As general comments usually bring more clarity about the contents of the right, they could have an influence on the recognition of the self – executing character of the CRC-provisions by the national courts. They could also lead to a broader stand-still effect of the provisions and may help detect the negative States' obligations.

---

[202] In General Comment No 1, for instance, the Committee formulated some new reporting requirements.

[203] K. Arambulo, *Strengthening the Supervision of the International Covenant on Economic, Social and Cultural Rights, Theoretical and Procedural Aspects* (Antwerpen/Groningen/Oxford, Intersentia-Hart), 1999, p. 161.

[204] G. Van Bueren, *o.c.* (note 5), pp. 388 and 411.

[205] Iwasawa, for instance, points out that general comments adopted under the conventions ratified by Japan have been invoked before Japanese courts, see Y. Iwasawa, *l.c.* (note 201), p. 259.

CHAPTER FIVE

THE EFFECTIVENESS OF THE REPORTING PROCEDURE

53. The success of the reporting procedure depends on several interrelated factors,[206] such as (a) the willingness of the governments to fulfil their reporting obligations in an accurate way: *i.e.* in time and submitting a report of good quality, (b) the quality of the dialogue, (c) the quality of the concluding observations, (d) an accurate follow-up by the States, (e) the independence of the Committee, (f) financial and human resources within the UN Secretariat, and (g) the involvement of NGOs and the media in the reporting process. From what has been outlined above, it is clear that some issues of concern exist in this regard.

54. Before listing the main problems the CRC Committee is confronted with, it should be noted that these are part of the general difficulty the UN human rights treaty system is in. Since more than a decade, a lot of attention has been paid to the efficiency of this system and many recommendations, both short-term and long-term, were made in order to provide some kind of remedy.[207]

55. A mayor problem the Committee is facing is the volume of work, attended by a lack of time. This resulted in a still increasing delay between the submission of the reports and their examination.[208] A normal, acceptable lapse

---

[206] For an analysis of some of these factors, see J. Conners, 'An analyses and Evaluation of the System of State Reporting', in: A.F. Bayefsky (ed.), *The UN Human Rights System in the 21st Century* (The Hague/London/Boston, Kluwer Law International, 2000), pp. 3–21.

[207] The UN itself, well aware of the unsustainability of the system, appointed an independent expert to carry out a study in order to remedy the current situation. The latter submitted its final recommendations in 1996: Ph. Alston, *Effective functioning of Bodies established pursuant to United Nations human rights instruments. Final report on enhancing the long-term effectiveness of the United Nations human rights treaty system, o.c.* (note 127), 20p.; Also a lot of scholars put forward some ideas for structural change: see *e.g.* Ph. Alston and J. Crawford, *The future of UN Human Rights Treaty Monitoring*, Cambridge (Cambridge University Press, 2000), 563p; A.F. Bayefsky (ed.), *The UN Human Rights System in the 21st Century* (The Hague/London/Boston, Kluwer Law International, 2000), pp. 1–341; and A.F. Bayefsky, *The United Nations Human Rights Treaty System. Universality at the Crossroads* (The Hague/London/New York, Kluwer Law International, 2001), pp. 1–180.

[208] J. Crawford, 'The UN Human Rights Treaty System: A system in crisis?', in: Ph. Alston and J. Crawford (eds.), *The future of UN Human Rights Treaty Monitoring* (Cambridge, Cambridge University Press, 2000), p. 5.

of time between the submission of the report and its examination in the pre-sessional working group is nine to twelve months.[209] However, in most cases this period is much longer and can even be two years or more. As has been stated above, the Committee took some measures in this regard and made efforts to spend its available time as efficiently as possible.[210] However, in spite of these measures, the Committee will never be able to completely get rid of the backlog. As will be the case for all the treaty bodies, radical changes will have to be carried through. Alston listed several options available to deal with these problems and made some recommendations.[211] Amongst other things, he proposed to eliminate the requirement that the periodic reports should be comprehensive. As mentioned earlier, the Committee has announced to respond to this proposal by revising its general guidelines for periodic reporting.[212] A second measure suggested by Alston is a consolidation of treaty bodies. Also the American Bar Association is in favour of such a consolidation: it advocates the replacement of the existing UN treaty Committees by two consolidated Committees: one on States Parties' reports and one on complaints. This would mean that the States Parties would have only one consolidated report rather than the six many of them have to submit under the current system.[213] These proposals can however only be considered as long-term projects. In the meanwhile, it is up to the Committee to seek further creative solutions and it remains to be seen what the result will be of the foreseen split into two chambers.

56. Some other concerns relate to the cooperation of the governments. Firstly, a lot of States are years behind in submitting their reports, others simply do not report.[214] As of January 2005, the website of the Office of the High Commissioner for Human Rights mentions a total of 129 overdue reports for the CRC itself; 43 for the Optional Protocol on the involvement of children in armed conflict, and 46 for the Optional Protocol on the sale of

---

[209] UN Doc. CRC/C/SR.858, 2003, para. 39.

[210] *Cf. supra* No 34.

[211] Ph. Alston, *Effective functioning of Bodies established pursuant to United Nations human rights instruments. Final report on enhancing the long-term effectiveness of the United Nations human rights treaty system, o.c.* (note 127), paras. 85–101.

[212] *Cf. supra* No 24.

[213] American Bar Association (ABA), 'Recommendation towards consolidating into two committees the existing six UN committees currently monitoring UN human rights treaties (CCPR, CESR, CERD, CEDAW, CAT, CRC)', *Human Rights Journal* 20, Nos. 4–6, 1999, p. 274.

[214] J. Crawford, *l.c.* (note 208), pp. 4–5; According to Alston, there are two reasons why States do not report: administrative incapacity and lack of political will. The same author states that raising the costs of non-compliance might constitute a solution to this problem: see Ph. Alston, *Effective functioning of Bodies established pursuant to United Nations human rights*

children child prostitution and child pornography.[215] In 2002, the Committee responded to this problem in a recommendation allowing for exceptional submission of combined reports.[216] If a report is due within a year after the dialogue or at the time of the dialogue on the previous report, States Parties are allowed to submit together with the next report. In order to avoid further delay in the examination of the report once submitted, the Committee asks to submit 18 months earlier than this second deadline.[217] This rule is exceptional and applies for one time only. It attempts to provide an opportunity for negligent States Parties to respect the strict reporting periodicity.

In case of persistent neglect, the standard censure is that the Committee sends several reminders and when these are not replied to, it refers to the delays in its annual report to the UN General Assembly.[218] The latter then can decide to call the delinquent States to fulfil their duties. However, as Crawford states, these calls are so far ineffectual.[219] The same author stresses that 'the system, established to oversee State compliance, depends for its continued functioning on a high level of State default'.[220] The huge backlog in State reporting might at the moment be considered as a blessing for the Committee rather than a problem. But, as Alston says, 'this is hardly a satisfactory foundation upon which to build an effective and efficient monitoring system'.[221] Therefore, he recommends that 'in responding to cases of persistent delinquency, all treaty bodies should be urged to adopt procedures which lead to the examination of situations even in the absence of a report'.[222] The Committee followed this advice by personally addressing the most negligent States. Those States which had to submit their reports in 1992, 1993 or 1994 are requested to do so within a year. In case they fail to do so the Committee made clear that it will examine the children's rights

---

instruments. Final report on enhancing the long-term effectiveness of the United Nations human rights treaty system, o.c. (note 127), paras. 43–46. It should also be mentioned that the States have had to draw up increasingly more reports since the last years. It is consequently harder for the national administrations to submit the various reports in due time.

[215] http://www.ohchr.org/.

[216] CRC Committee, Recommendation on the Organization of Work (UN Doc. CRC/C/114, 2002), p. 5.

[217] CRC Committee, Recommendation on the Organization of Work (UN Doc. CRC/C/124, 2003), pp. 4–5.

[218] CRC Committee, the Provisional Rules of Procedure (UN Doc. CRC/C/4, 1991), Rule 67.

[219] J. Crawford, l.c. (note 208), p. 4.

[220] Ibid., p. 6; See also Ph. Alston, Effective functioning of Bodies established pursuant to United Nations human rights instruments. Final report on enhancing the long-term effectiveness of the United Nations human rights treaty system, o.c. (note 127), para. 48.

[221] Ph. Alston, Effective functioning of Bodies established pursuant to United Nations human rights instruments. Final report on enhancing the long-term effectiveness of the United Nations human rights treaty system, o.c. (note 127), para. 48.

[222] Ibid., para. 112 and paras. 37–47.

situation in the country on the basis of other sources. This pressure seems to have positive effects, since several States reacted by eventually submitting their report.[223]

Secondly, there is the often voiced criticism that country reports are not reliable because of the fact that they are drawn up by national officials, who try to describe as positive as possible the situation of children in their countries and often conceal flagrant violations of human rights. It is therefore important for the effectiveness of the reporting procedure that the Committee can gather additional information, also from other sources.[224] As has been pointed out above, the Committee makes good use of the NGO input and the information it receives from other UN organs. The Committee even took the initiative to enhance the participation of other organs in the reporting procedure.[225] However, in spite of these important advances, there remain some problems as to the participation of NGOs in the reporting process. NGOs indeed do not participate directly in the dialogue between the Committee and the States whose reports are being considered. NGO's do not get the chance to refute the answers of the government representatives.[226] Furthermore, Clapham points at the fact that due to the lack of time, money and secretariat staff, the NGO information is too often not sufficiently studied.[227] It is up to the Committee to pave the way for more meaningful interaction with NGOs during and after the examination of the reports.

57. Furthermore, there exist some aspects of concern regarding the Committee members: the election are too often politicised[228] and most of the members have a full time job next to their commitment to the Committee. This often leads to their absence, especially at the pre-sessional working group and inadequate time to spend preparing the meetings.[229]

58. It goes without saying that also the lack of resources, yielding to an understaffed secretariat, restrictions on translations and limited technology affect the activities of the Committee in a negative way.[230]

---

[223] UN Docs. CRC/C/114, 2002, para. 561; CRC/C/130, 2003, para. 4; and CRC/C/141, 2004, paras. 8–9. See also UN Docs. CRC/C/33, 1994, paras. 29–32; and CRC/C/4, 1991, Rule 67.
[224] See V. Dimitrijevic, *l.c.* (note 77), pp. 192 and 195–197; and A.H. Robertson and J.G. Merrills, *Human Rights in the world - An introduction to the study of the international protection of human rights* (Manchester/New York, Manchester University Press), 1992, p. 41.
[225] *Cf. supra* Nos. 41–43 and No 29.
[226] A. Clapham, *l.c.* (note 109), p. 187.
[227] *Ibid.*, p. 188.
[228] J. Crawford, *l.c.* (note 208), p. 9.
[229] A. Clapham, *l.c.* (note 109), pp. 188–190.
[230] J. Crawford, *l.c.* (note 208), p. 7.

59. Next to the problems related to the dependencies of the reporting mechanism, some criticism is voiced with regard to its non-judicial nature. Indeed, when looking at the monitoring system from a juridical angle, and when checking the degree to which the victim of a violation of human rights can call in the support of the Committee to cease the violation, one cannot but conclude that the control mechanism of the CRC offers only few possibilities. Until today, victims can not file an individual complaint, States Parties who do not submit their report (in time) are not censured and the concluding observations of the Committee cannot be enforced. Although intentions were uttered to start debating the establishment of an individual complaints procedure under the CRC,[231] at the moment no progress is made in this regard and a lot thus still depends on the good-will of the States themselves.

60. Another often voiced criticism on the reporting procedure concerns the fact that the Committee is only authorised to act when it has a report at its disposal. Although some evolution has occurred in theory (*i.e.* the possibility for the Committee to take urgent actions),[232] in practice, the Committee almost never takes action outside the reporting cycle.

61. In spite of the harsh but often justifiable criticism on the use and the effectiveness of the reporting procedure, the latter has its own advantages and record of successes.

The reporting system appears to be 'the' method to monitor the fulfilment of human rights obligations on a broad scale. It does not depart from violations of rights but instead acts on a non-casuistic basis by overseeing the implementation of the CRC as a whole. It performs this task through awareness raising, education and dialogue. In this way the Committee aims to come to a universal culture of rights.[233] It raises awareness of the existence and the meaning of the rights of the child amongst law and policy makers, and in the community as a whole. In this context, the Committee encour-

---

[231] *Cf. Supra* note 27. For the moment, the CRC Committee limits its efforts in this regard by encouraging children or their representatives to refer to other treaty bodies, which receive individual complaints.

[232] *Cf. supra* Nos. 44–47.

[233] *I.e.* 'one in which the actual meaning of rights and their implications for specific individuals and groups are commonly understood and internalised by governments and civil society alike': see J. Karp, *l.c.* (note 83), p. 37.

ages the States to publish the concluding observations made to their reports.[234] The importance of human rights education has also been stressed by the drafters of the CRC by including an obligation for the governments to make the principles and the provisions of the CRC[235] as well as their reports widely available to the public.[236] The way of working of the Committee can also be called large-scale in the sense that it involves all interested parties. The government itself is obliged to make a periodical self-evaluation. The civil society – including children themselves – and other interested bodies get a forum to publicly scrutinise and discuss State activity.[237] In this way, a cooperative, coordinated and holistic way of implementation becomes possible.

62. The direct impact of the CRC and its reporting procedure on domestic law-making and policy and on the actions of NGOs and other civil society actors, is difficult to determine. This requires a profound analyses of the government's behaviour with regard to the fulfilment of its CRC obligations, including its response to the recommendations of the Committee on the one hand and of the civil society's actions on the other hand. Generally it can be stated that, following the recommendations of the Committee, some initiatives were taken by governments in order to improve the implementation of the rights of the child; in this sense inter-ministerial committees and ombudsmen for children were introduced. Other responses by the governments are annual reports to the parliament, child impact statements, closer cooperation with NGOs, interdepartmental cooperation etc. The Committee also influenced the civil society, mainly through the creation of NGO coalitions and more generally by increasing the NGO involvement in promoting and monitoring children's rights.[238] Until today, studies that thoroughly assess the effect of the CRC and its implementation system are rare.[239] It might be a future challenge to do some further research on the impact of the Convention. It is however never possible to exactly examine to what

[234] UN Doc. CRC/C/20, 1993, para. 29.
[235] Article 42 of the CRC.
[236] Article 44(6) of the CRC.
[237] J. Conners, l.c. (note 206), p. 7.
[238] L. Woll, *The Convention on the Rights of the Child Impact Study* (Växjö, Save the Children Sweden, 2000), p. 26; see also G. Lansdown, l.c. (note 109), pp. 120–122.
[239] L. Woll, o.c. (note 238), 251 p.; In this study, six country case studies are made in which the practical impact of the CRC was examined.

degree a monitoring system can have a positive influence on human rights: 'too many factors influence progress in human rights to make it possible to document precisely the role of international supervisory systems'.[240] Identifying the origin of law reform (and its implementation) and tracing the source of certain measures and practices is very complex, time-consuming and in a lot of occasions impossible. Moreover, as realising children's rights is seen as a gradual process, the impact can often only be assessed in the long run. In this sense, the required mind shift in order to consider children as subjects of rights instead of pure objects of legal protection is a gradual and long-term process in which the reporting procedure can act as a catalyst.

The question as to the direct impact of the CRC and its reporting procedure on the life of children, is even more difficult to answer. As WOLL states, the causal connection between *e.g.* a decrease in child poverty and the ratification of the CRC or the reporting obligation cannot be proved.[241]

63. It should be stressed that the non-judicial nature of the reporting process does not mean that the CRC would have no juridical meaning at all. Firstly, the self-executing force of some rights was recognised by the domestic courts in several States.[242] In this respect, the elaboration of general comments by the Committee can play an important role.[243] Secondly, the Convention itself as well as the activities of the Committee could lead to further national or regional standard setting.

64. Finally, it may once again be underlined that the Committee has been quite creative in developing its working methods, which resulted in a fairly efficient procedure. In this sense the beneficial partnership between the Committee and other bodies, inside and outside the UN, is partly due to the Committee's efforts to enforce this cooperation. Together with the Committee's reporting guidelines and recommendations on simplifying the State reports, this cooperation facilitates a comprehensive impression of the children's

---

[240] A. Virginia Leary, 'Lessons from the Experience of the International Labour Organisation', in: Ph. Alston (ed.), *The United Nations and Human Rights. A Critical Appraisal* (Oxford, Clarendon Press, 1992), p. 595.

[241] L. Woll, *o.c.* (note 238), p. 12.

[242] See for instance A. Vandaele and W. Pas, 'International Human Rights Treaties and their relation with National Law: Monism, Dualism, and the Self-executing Character of Human Rights', in: E. Verhellen and A. Weyts (eds.), *Understanding Children's Rights–2003* (Children's Rights Centre, Ghent University, Ghent, 2004), pp. 384–393.

[243] *Cf. supra* No 52.

rights situation in a particular country, being the basis for an efficient mon-itory procedure. Furthermore, its emphasis on the national dimension of the reporting procedure, and its requests for international cooperation based on Article 45(b) are quite innovative, and contribute to the realisation of the Committee's recommendations at the domestic level.

65. To conclude it can be said that the monitoring system, provided for by the CRC, can, by means of awareness – raising, education and dialogue, be an important tool in the process of realising the rights of the child. At the same time it cannot be denied that it is a system with various constraints, which requires continual attention to prevent it from becoming a superfi-cial ceremony.